NEW HEAVEN, NEW EARTH

PAVILION SERIES
General Editor: F. G. Bailey

NEW HEAVEN
NEW EARTH

A Study of Millenarian Activities

KENELM BURRIDGE

Fellow of St Cross College, Oxford

PAVILION SERIES

SOCIAL ANTHROPOLOGY

OXFORD
BASIL BLACKWELL
1971

© Basil Blackwell 1969
Reprinted 1971

631 11950 7 Paper bound edition
631 11960 4 Cloth bound edition

Library of Congress Catalog Card No.:
69–20429

Printed in Great Britain by
Compton Printing Ltd London and Aylesbury
and bound by the Kemp Hall Bindery, Oxford

Contents

vi *Contents*

Preface

This essay is a development of four lectures given at the University of Sussex in the Spring of 1967 at the invitation of Professor F. G. Bailey. Professor Bailey asked me to provide young anthropologists, as well as scholars in other disciplines and the interested layman, with a general conspectus of the problems involved in the study of millenarian movements. This I have tried to do within the terms of a particular point of view. But there seems little point to an essay that does not provoke. So, rather than review the main landmarks in an enormous body of literature, I have sought to incorporate appreciation and criticism within a specific approach and synthesis. Whilst the coverage is reasonably wide, I have tried to raise problems rather than solve them. Though most of the examples have been taken from the evidence provided by the simpler communities that most anthropologists study, some balance has been achieved with examples from more complex communities. My object has been to widen, not narrow, the perspectives offered by millenarian movements.

My thanks go to Professor Bailey both for providing the opportunity and for his help in preparing the manuscript. I dedicate the book to those reading anthropology at the University of Sussex.

K.O.L.B.

St Cross College, Oxford

1
Introduction

The title of this essay is one way of describing what is meant by 'millennium'. And, accepting an anthropological viewpoint, it attempts to discuss answers to three main questions:

(a) What is the meaning of the millennium to those who participate in millenarian activities?

(b) How may anthropologists so frame their questions about millenarian activities that answers to them can be obtained from the empirical fieldwork material?

(c) How may we extract the sociology of these activities from the contingencies of their historical matrix?

Answers to the first question seem at first glance simple. They are reached by intuitive means, by an empathic understanding of what one has seen or read of millenarian activities. But there are difficulties. Some participants may see the activities as a vehicle of spiritual salvation; and others may seem more concerned for their own immediate material advantage. To decide which of these two meanings is more useful or correct or true it becomes necessary to contest an explicit conceptual system. Otherwise differences of opinion must remain personal and subjective if not trivial. In short, to extract a 'meaning' that has some 'objective' validity, which takes account of but transcends varieties of particular motives and rationalizations, the answers to the first question must depend on the sorts of answers given to the other two.

Finding out what actually happens or happened in a millenarian movement and then constructing an historical narrative is clearly the first step. After further investigation it may become possible to show some sorts of coherence between the historical events and the patterns of social relations. But that fusion of historical events and social relations into a statement valid for both participants and investigator as well as for other similar situations elsewhere and at other times still presents difficulties. An old problem[1] which was laid on one side[2] for a number of years but never forgotten[3] as anthropologists grappled with the ethnographic present—the attempt to show abiding logical principle in social relations—it has again begun to receive serious attention.[4] Within the context of this theoretical probing and rethinking, as anthropologists begin to handle 'social change' and 'developmental processes' more expertly, developing new ways of interpreting the materials of history, the study of millenarian activities assumes a prime importance. They provide a test case. They occur as historical events over a relatively short time; they involve changes in social relations; they tend to predicate changes in social organization as well as in what some think of as social structure.[5] Beyond their intrinsic human interest, that is, millenarian activities constitute an acute theoretical challenge. They invite a statement through which particular actions and rationalizations may be given a more general validity.

This essay attempts a preliminary clearing of the ground. It surveys the problems involved by discussing particular examples; then it attempts a break-down and re-synthesis of the components of various types of millenarian activity. It is exploratory, posing problems rather than solving them.

[1] See for example the works of Hegel, Compte, Marx, Herbert Spencer, Marc Bloch, and Fustel de Coulanges among many others.

[2] Mainly through the influence of Bronislaw Malinowski and A. R. Radcliffe-Brown. See *Jarvie* (2) where the case is perhaps overstated.

[3] See *Schapera*, where he gives many examples.

[4] One thinks particularly of *Evans-Pritchard* (2) (*Essays in Social Anthropology*, pp. 13–28); *Leach* (1), (2); *Pocock*; *Martindale*; *Goldschmidt*.

[5] On another view (e.g. *Lévi-Strauss* (1), pp. 1–25; 277–313) 'structure' is a particular kind of sociological analysis which is quite irreconcilable with historical analysis.

2
Opening the Problem

To dream a dream and make it come true; to realize the shape of
what can be seen only in the mind's eye; to feel compelled to
bring about the seemingly impossible—these are the preroga-
tives of man. James Naylor was ploughing his fields when, in a
blinding and timeless moment, he knew why he had been born.
Like Saint Paul, who never wavered in his adherence to a truth
revealed to him in a vision, James Naylor, despite the cruelties
of parliament and a bigoted religious orthodoxy, remained
steadfast in what his vision had revealed to him. Driven by her
voices, a French peasant girl put new life into a dispirited army
and routed the alien invader. She was burned at the stake as a
heretic and witch; she was also canonized Saint Joan. Ann Lee
claimed to be the new Christ; Joseph Smith had a vision of
heavenly bliss to be realized in an earthly community life; and
thousands of miles and moments away a Maori, a Papuan, an
African, an Indian—each is impelled to tell his good news of a
new way of life. Whether as fool, fraud, saint, respectable bour-
geois, farmer or tycoon, the pain of the millennium belongs only
to man. It is why he is man, why, when the time comes, he has
to make a new man.

Some fifty years ago Haddon wrote:[1] 'An awakening of religious activity is a frequent characteristic of periods of social
unrest. The weakening or disruption of the old social order may
stimulate new and often bizarre ideals, and these may give rise
to religious movements that strive to sanction social and political aspirations. Communities that feel themselves oppressed
anticipate the emergence of a hero who will restore their prosperity and prestige. And when the people are imbued with religious fervour the expected hero will be regarded as a Messiah.
Phenomena of this kind are well known in history, and are not

[1] *Chinnery and Haddon*, p. 455.

unknown at the present day among peoples in all stages of civilization.'

A forceful and succinct enough statement. In the space of a paragraph Haddon describes the kind of activity we are setting out to examine. It is worthwhile going over it to make sure we know what we mean by some of the words Haddon uses.

RELIGION AND REDEMPTION

What we mean by 'religious activity' is clearly of key importance. Writing at the time he did Haddon may have had in mind Tylor's minimal definition of religion: 'the belief in spiritual beings'.[1] Or, since it is more usual and puts more generally much the same point as Tylor made more specifically, it may be that Haddon thought of 'religious activity' as essentially defined by a belief in the supernatural. But neither of these definitions is of much sociological value as they stand. For though we can observe rites and rituals and infer their symbolic references with some accuracy, the problem of belief begs the question, we cannot know what a spiritual being is without further qualification, and it is too often tempting to define a belief in the supernatural in terms that would scarcely apply to anybody anywhere.[2] We need a broader view, one that subsumes the variety of activities that may be religious.

Meditating on the infinite may be a religious activity, so may writing a cheque, eating corpses, copulating, listening to a thumping sermon on hell fire, examining one's conscience, painting a picture, growing a beard, licking leprous sores, tying the body into knots, a dogged faith in human rationality—there is no human activity which cannot assume religious significance. When it does so it has overriding importance. It points to that which permeates and informs a whole way of life, and, more

---

[1] *Tylor*, p. 424.

[2] If a 'spiritual being' is expressly not human, it still must involve questions as to mass, visibility, and attributes of bilocation. Not to 'believe in' phenomena such as trances, stigmata, possession, levitation, walking on hot coals without being burned, or skewering the cheeks without leaving a wound—which are all above or beyond the natural, not found in nature—is surely equivalent to being a 'flat-earther'.

crucially, it indicates sources or principles of power which are regarded as particularly creative or destructive.[1] Indeed, all religions are basically concerned with power. They are concerned with the discovery, identification, moral relevance and ordering of different kinds of power whether these manifest themselves as thunder, or lightning, atomic fission, untrammelled desire, arrogance, impulse, apparitions, visions, or persuasive words. Within these terms a spiritual being, whether thought of as a deity or ghost or human being or angel or goblin or fairy, becomes a named and identified source or principle of power with particular and often measurable attributes and ranges of power.[2] And all that is meant by a belief in the supernatural is the belief that there do exist kinds of power whose manifestations and effects are observable, but whose natures are not yet fully comprehended.

Religions, let us say, are concerned with the systematic ordering of different kinds of power, particularly those seen as significantly beneficial or dangerous. This entails a specific framework of rules. But because a religion is concerned with the truth of things, and reaches out to discover and identify those sorts of power which, though sensed and affective, are currently not wholly comprehended, its rules about the use and control of different kinds of powers are grounded in an interplay between experience, working assumptions, and those more rooted assumptions we call faith. As experience widens and deepens, some of the rules and assumptions will be qualified, and others abandoned altogether—a developmental process in which received truths or assumptions give way to new truths, and in which the new truths become in their turn the received assumptions of future generations. These assumptions are community truths, truths which command a consensus. From them are derived the sets of moral imperatives, obligations, and rules of conduct to which men,

[1] When we say of a man that 'art is his religion' we mean that he gives overriding importance to art, that he is particularly concerned with nurturing and developing his sources of inspiration, and guarding himself against those influences which might endanger his inspiration, betray his integrity as an artist, or nullify his ideas on what Art should be or do. The same applies to those of whom we might say 'science is his religion', or 'socialism is his religion', or 'anthropology is his religion'.

[2] This holds even though it might be said that a 'spiritual being' is but the rationalized projection of some internal impulse.

because they live in community, subject themselves. Yet though man governs his condition with explicit and articulate rules of this kind, they are rarely interconsistent. Concrete situations often involve selecting one rule at the expense of another, and individuals, whether selfishly or otherwise motivated, accord differing priorities to some obligations at the expense of others. And here too we touch on the essence of religious activity. For, given a context determined by current assumptions about power, the process whereby individuals attempt to discharge their obligations in relation to the moral imperatives of the community is no less than a 'redemptive process'.

From the pen of a social scientist, 'redemptive process' seems a curious phrase. But it is useful. The human condition appears as one of general indebtedness: a feature which we acknowledge in variations of the aphorism 'paying our debt to society'. For whether the capacities of a human being are given him by God and/or a particular combination of genes, his potential can only be realized after a long process of feeding, nurturing, teaching and training by parents and others. Society, moreover, prescribes the attitudes and activities by which its members can pay back or redeem the debt incurred in being nurtured, made morally aware, and enabled to exert and realize their potential. While these prescribed activities may be thought of as 'redemptive media', the media through which the debt is repaid or redeemed, the process of engaging in the activities—activities which are ordered in terms of particular kinds of obligations—is, in our idiom, the redemptive process, a process which leads on to redemption itself. But this, the payment of the debt in full, can only be realized when a human being becomes in himself completely unobliged, without any obligation whatsoever—a free-mover in heaven, enjoying nirvana, or joined with the ancestors. For since existence in community, a moral order, necessarily entails existence within a network of obligations, redemption itself can only be realized at or after that appropriate death which brings to an end an appropriate mode of discharging one's obligations.

We may now move towards a working definition of religion and religious activity. Let us say that they refer to

The redemptive process indicated by the activities, moral rules, and assumptions about power which, pertinent to the moral order and

taken on faith, not only enable a people to perceive the truth of things, but guarantee that they are indeed perceiving the truth of things.[1]

This definition has several advantages. Instead of tucking religion into an obscure and even almost irrelevant compartmen of social life, we give it the overriding importance it actually seems to have. For not only are religions concerned with the truth about power, but the reverse also holds: a concern with the truth about power is a religious activity. Operationally, this concern is expressed in maintaining or challenging the rules which govern the use and control of power. And these rules assume the form of a set of moral discriminations which, in constricting animal man, also provide him with opportunities for realizing his moral nature and potential. The definition implies, and therefore leads us to expect—despite the conservatism of particular religious orthodoxies—that religious activities will change when the asumptions about the nature of power, and hence the rules which govern its use and control, can no longer guarantee the truth of things.

The use of this definition spares us unnecessary wrangling with distinctions between religion and magic. We are not led into the impasse of calling the religions of other peoples bundles of superstitions. We are insulated from the prejudgements contained in the dichotomies rational/irrational and secular/religious. If a general rationality and order among human beings and their affairs are not assumed from the start, sociological analysis must founder. The label 'irrational' tends to become a portmanteau of ethnocentric prejudices, for faith is faith whether thought of as religious or secular. More positively, with this definition we can identify activities and movements of generally millenarian type where the words 'God', 'deity', or 'spiritual being' or their synonyms in other languages are not in evidence. Because politics, too, are concerned with power, it becomes clear and explicit that no religious movement lacks a political ideology. And, accepting the political significance, we are forced to look at the ways in which wealth is distributed, and we must take account of what powers are dependent on various kinds of wealth.

If it is not to become overly ethnocentric, anthropology or

[1] Cf. *Lienhardt*, pp. 327–9; *Yinger*, pp. 9, 71–2; *Vernon*, pp. 46–57; *Horton*.

comparative sociology must, initially, use broad concepts capable of containing the varied arrangements offered by different cultures. The 'redemptive process' is just such a concept. Not necessarily hedged with mystery, it is something we can observe, ask about, talk about. The rules which govern the use of power can be determined. Both emerge from the ways in which individuals discharge or evade their obligations, what they do to counter or meet the consequences of evasion, how they cope with a pledge redeemed, what they say the consequences will or might be. We can, too, identify preliminary or temporary states of redemption.[1] Finally, we can accept provisionally the crude formula, Salvation = Redemption = Unobligedness, or release from all obligations. For, by examining the kinds of redemption or releases from obligation that are offered by particular kinds of millenarian activity, we might be able to see more accurately what assumptions and rules are currently not revealing the truth of things, what kinds of redemptive process would be more in tune with an actual or desired distribution of power.

NEW IDEALS

It will be clear from what has been said above that 'periods of social unrest' and the 'weakening or disruption of the old social order' refer to situations where the relevant assumptions about power are weakening and no longer enable individuals to perceive the truth of things. They cannot project a satisfactory redemptive process. Hence the 'new and often bizarre ideals'. These may be seen as attempts to reformulate assumptions about power so that they may account for the widening experiences of everyday life and provide the basis for a new mode of redemption. New ideals, new assumptions certainly. But whether or not they are bizarre is entirely subjective. No one, it may be assumed, does seriously what he himself thinks is bizarre. Just as other kinds of seeming strange and esoteric activities in foreign cultures have yielded their mystery to

[1] See, for example, *Burridge* (5), pp. 226–9, where a New Guinea people, after a series of reciprocal exchanges or discharges of obligation, attain to a state known as *mngwotngwotiki*, a word which connotes a particular field of relations in which the individuals concerned are temporarily unobliged to each other.

investigation, so again and again the apparently bizarre in millenarian movements has been shown to be unexceptionable in the circumstances, given the premises. The hypothesis that millenary activities predicate a new culture or social order coming into being—which is what Haddon implies when he speaks of these movements as sanctioning 'social and political aspirations'—is a fair one. Certainly it is more scientific to regard these activities as new-cultures-in-the-making, or as attempts to make a new kind of society or moral community, rather than as oddities, diseases in the body social, or troublesome nuisances to efficient administration—though of course they may be all these as well.

Finally, of course, a millenarian movement is a new religion in the making. New assumptions are being ordered into what may become a new orthodoxy.

OPPRESSION

Haddon wrote in the heyday of British Imperial and colonial power. Despite the purposeful widening of the problem in the last sentence—which is often left out when authors quote him —it is fair to say that most anthropologists have understood by 'oppressed' simply the effects of the machinery of colonial expansion and government. The vast bulk of anthropological evidence has been drawn from the colonial situation: the effects of the activities of missionaries, traders, settlers, commercial enterprises and administrative bodies upon subject peoples; the whole business of a sophisticated, often greedy, and highly technological civilization imposing its rules and conventions and experience upon those who, hitherto, had led a relatively simple life in small communities based upon hunting, fishing, agriculture and handicrafts. Such evidence may well give a distorted impression, and it is useful to bear in mind that 'oppression' does not necessarily come from outside a particular cultural boundary. A people or group may oppress themselves and may only afterwards direct their frustrations at outsiders.[1] Hence perhaps Haddon's telling phrase: 'Communities that *feel* (my italics) themselves oppressed . . .' Further, it should not be thought that the word 'oppressed' could refer to anything more

[1] Below, pp. 92–4.

than what we have identified already: traditional assumptions weakening, a moral order decaying, a positive and active if not always apparently sober will to participate in wider or different categories of understanding whether these are phrased in economic or political or more mystical terms. 'Feeling themselves oppressed' by current assumptions about power, participants in millenarian activities set themselves the task of reformulating their assumptions so as to create, or account for and explain, a new or changing material and moral environment within which a more satisfactory form of redemption will be obtained.

HEROES

The 'emergence of a hero' touches the well-springs of an abundant literature. We can afford to be brief. If he is to be accepted as such, a hero or prophet or messiah must make his presence known to the community that is expecting him; and in order to be recognized and enabled to communicate with his followers he must conform in some way to the popular image of a hero or prophet or messiah. Since existing authorities are quick to scent a challenge, it is only prudent to gain the support of respected leaders of the community without appearing as a rival to them; and this an emerging hero can only do if what he has to say expresses and articulates just those questions which the community feels disturbed and anxious about. Further, he should provide clear and acceptable answers or solutions to the questions being asked. Is acceptance really dependent on Haddon's rather vague 'religious fervour'? Perhaps. But even if observers of the scene were competent to analyse effectively the hysteria and similar emotional disturbances which accompany many a millenarian movement, within the terms of our view of religion we can see that many other more accessible and as relevant features enter into the developing situation: differences in economic and political circumstances; variations in capacities and opportunities as between millenarian group and others; impasses of communication and understanding.

Nonetheless, providing that we understand by 'religious fervour' not simply an emotional exhibition, but a state-of-being having sociological relevance, it is an important phrase. New assumptions which predicate the creation of a new man, a new culture, society or condition of being are being wrought. And these relate directly to 'prosperity and prestige'—though not necessarily to a restoration of traditional kinds of prosperity and prestige. The new assumptions tend to meet in the hero and his (divine) revelation, and almost always refer to a 'prosperity and prestige' that are consistent with, and even define, the new conditions of being, the new man. As we shall see, an adequate or more satisfactory way of gaining prestige, of defining the criteria by which the content of manhood is to be measured, stands at the very heart of a millennarian or messianic movement. And these criteria relate on the one hand to gaining or retaining self-respect, status, and that integrity which is implied in the approved retention of a particular status; and on the other hand to an acknowledged process whereby redemption may be won.

Logically, a messianic movement is one that requires a messiah. And so accustomed are we to a 'movement' having a leader or hero or prophet that we tend to forget that some millenarian activities may take place without one. There must have been many episodes or occurrences in history, as there certainly have been in Oceania in recent times,[1] which, lacking one who could be identified as a leader, still evoke new assumptions and are otherwise of the same genre as those more coherently organized activities in which some kind of hero or prophet or messiah has been identified. In such cases, one may say, the new assumptions are implicit rather than explicit. The messiah or hero or prophet is but an emerging idea, unrealized as yet in the flesh.

PROPHETS

There is no need to say much about the words 'messiah', 'hero', 'prophet', 'chiliastic', 'millenarian', 'messianic', 'cult', 'movement', 'activities'. To think that each term refers to a distinct person or situation obscures rather than clarifies, closes rather than opens the sociological problem. Only when the activities have been made to yield to a general conceptual framework may we go on to distinguish different types. Thus although outside the Judaeo-Christian-Islamic traditions there can in the

---

[1] See *Burridge* (3), pp. 1–4.

strict sense be no prophets, messiahs or messianic traditions or expectations—though there may well be traditions of a messianic type, and many whom we could say were heroes—we shall use the word prophet to refer to the leader, prime mover, star or central personality in the kinds of activities we are discussing. Chiliastic, millenarian and messianic will be regarded as synonymous terms; and whether the activities constitute a cult or a movement the reader may decide for himself.[1] Such usage does not prejudge any useful distinctions there might be between these terms, but it does avoid argument as to whether a person was really a hero or messiah or false or true prophet before we are in a position to make the argument worthwhile. Being ourselves the children of a long-established tradition of messianic expectations there are advantages in using familiar terms, opportunities only for confusion in adding to the plethora of nomenclatures invented over recent years.[2]

On the other hand, temptations to seize on similarities at the expense of differences should be resisted. As we shall see, there are pertinent differences between one kind of millenarian activity and another. There are also different kinds of prophet—a half-crazed woman obsessed with her visions, for example, or a sickly lad who dreams a dream upon which others act, but who himself is heard of no more; a shrewd man of stature with organizing ability; a visionary or seer given to trances; or a saintly man misled by his own piety. Further, at least in the preliminary stages before a movement has cohered, there may be no prophet at all—just a series of apparently impulsive activities accompanied by inchoate ideas, feelings and emotions. Only when the inchoate ideas have begun to cohere into new assumptions may a prophet emerge to articulate them, show them forth, make them explicit. This is the revelation which, thought of as divinely inspired, provides the basis for a new departure, a new mode of redemption.

Every millenarian movement for which we have evidence comes to us as a story, as a narration of historical or quasi-

---

[1] While 'activity' is a general descriptive term, one may suggest that a cult, concerned with a particular source of power, is already organized, firm and static, whereas a movement seeks to impose its ideas and present organization upon a wider field.

[2] Below, pp. 102–3.

historical events. Often, too, we find either *ad hoc* or systematic attempts to relate the events of the story to events and features of social relationship which lie outside the confines of the story itself. This, in essence, is what is meant by 'extracting the sociology from the history'. The issue is how satisfactorily, completely and systematically it may best be done. What we have attempted in developing each brief excursus above in terms of the content of others is a movement towards defining particular kinds of social relations in terms of the content of other kinds of social relations. We have rejected religion as simply a belief in spiritual beings; oppression as necessarily connoting the colonial situation; the prophet as a particular personality type. Instead, we have tried to make some interrelated statements about millenarian activities which can be filled out with empirical field-work material.

To summarize:

(a) We are discussing assumptions about power which, whether or not investigator or people concerned think of them as pertaining to spiritual beings, predicate or entail a particular redemptive process.

(b) While the redemptive process is discoverable in discharges and evasions of obligation, redemption itself refers to complete release from obligation and is roughly equivalent to salvation.

(c) The redemptive process, and so redemption, bears significantly on the politico-economic process, particularly the prestige system.

(d) A prestige system is based upon particular measurements of manhood which relate to gaining or retaining self-respect and integrity, and which refer back to the politico-economic process, the redemptive process, and assumptions about power.

Accepting these points as a baseline, millenarian movements involve the adoption of new assumptions, a new redemptive process, a new politico-economic framework, a new mode of measuring the man, a new integrity, a new community: in short, a new man. A precondition of this regeneration is a dissatisfaction with the current system. But if we describe this precondition as 'feeling oppressed', the 'oppression' does not necessarily derive from an external political control: it may be rooted in internal dissatisfactions with present assumptions, rules and modes of redemption. Either way, we are interested in the patterns described when faith belies experience, when given assumptions about power no longer reveal the truth of things, when the redemptive process must change to accord with the new assumptions born of new experience. When, as may happen, the new assumptions and rules are implicit and unorganized, millenarian activities may take place without a prophet being identifiable. A prophet is he or she who organizes the new assumptions and articulates them; who is listened to and found acceptable; whose revelation is accorded authority for however brief a period. But a prophet cannot identify himself in terms of the community as it is: he identifies himself in an image of what might or should be. When the prophet is missing we are like a detective investigating a murder without a motive, or a playwright whose characters are looking for a protagonist. Nevertheless, if we know something about the circumstances and their general pattern, we can make calculated guesses as to what might have been.

Sometimes the evidence at our disposal is thin. But this does not matter so long as our conceptual framework seems adequate to the information we have, and so long as it helps us to identify what we are looking for. Given these features, the framework itself may allow us to fill in some of the gaps.

3
Polynesian Illustrations

We now look at examples of the kinds of historical events we are trying to render sociologically intelligible. Most of them are taken from Oceania. This is not only because the bulk of the anthropological material comes from Oceania, but because the activities there make a variety of points relatively succinctly and enable us to tease out the detail most economically. The first group of three examples is concerned with Polynesians.

THE HAUHAU MOVEMENT, 1862[1]

The *Hauhau* movement of the Maori people of New Zealand arose directly from a prior movement known as the 'King movement', which was a purely political or administrative accommodation. Having become aware that white settlers were not temporary guests, but were taking or buying their hereditary lands and had come to stay, some of the Maori tribes between Taranaki and Waikato in the North Island confederated together under an elderly chief who took the title of King Potatau I. Not all the Maori in the area fully acknowledged the paramountcy of Potatau I, but he served as a rallying point and spokesman in disputes with white settlers and the not always scrupulous land agents of the colonial administration.[2] In the event King Potatau, a vacillating man whose title did not match his ability, could exert little authority. There were troubles, accidental deaths and murders, and consequent reprisals. And the punitive expeditions sent into the area by the European administration led to more reprisals by the Maori.

[1] Main sources are *Cowan*; *Babbage*; *Harrop*; *Greenwood*; *Winks*.
[2] All Maori tradition was against a paramountcy that had not been directly earned through feasts, gift giving, and war. A Chief had to command rather than beg for respect and obedience.

All these activities came to a head in the *Hauhau* or *Pai-marire*[1] movement. The founder of the movement was Te Ua (full name, Te Ua Horopapera Haumene), a man who in his youth had fought against white settlers, afterwards becoming a Christian and taking instruction from Christian missionaries. He was thought to be a lunatic, well known as subject to fits and trances. One day towards the end of 1862 or the beginning of 1863, Te Ua announced that the angel Gabriel had appeared to him in a vision. As a 'redemption for his people, who had become forgetful, desolate and in doubt',[2] Te Ua said, he would sacrifice his own son. Succeeding only in injuring the boy, Te Ua had another vision of the angel Gabriel and was instructed to take his son to a stream and bathe his wounds. A miraculous cure was reported, local Maori began to give Te Ua more serious attention. Now Te Ua, whose favourite work during his Christian period had been the Book of Revelations, announced that the angel Gabriel had revealed a new religion to him: the *Pai-marire*. The religion of England was false, said Te Ua. No notice should be taken of the Christian sabbath. Men and women should live promiscuously, so as to have children 'as the sands'. The priests of this new religion would have superhuman powers. Uttering the word *'Hau!'* would bring victory against the whites and recruit legions of angels who were waiting to help the Maori drive the Europeans into the sea. When the Europeans had gone, men from Heaven would teach the Maori all the arts and science of Europeans. By means of the spells, prayers and rituals which the angel Gabriel had revealed, Te Ua's followers would gain the gift of tongues and other miraculous powers. The priests would be able to teach English to adherents in one lesson.[3]

The central feature of *Pai-marire* ritual was a mast which had been salvaged from the *Lord Worsley*, a ship which had run ashore near Cape Egmont only a short while previously, and in the 'salvage' of whose cargo Te Ua had been involved. Crossed with a yard, rigged with stays and halliards and adorned with

[1] *Pai Marire* means 'Good and Peaceful'.
[2] *Winks*, p. 214. Quoting a document by the hand of Te Ua, captured by an English soldier, and published and translated in the *Taranaki Herald* on May 27th, 1865.
[3] *Harrop*, p. 217.

flags and pendants inscribed respectively with a St. George's cross, a St. Andrew's cross or cruciform, and the symbol ⊖,[1] the mast, set up in the village by the *marae* or traditional meeting place and burial ground, was known as a *niu*.[2] The rites themselves consisted of Te Ua or a leading disciple standing at the foot of the *niu* or mast inside a set of railings painted red, the followers circling around the pole, chanting hymns which Te Ua had taught them. The angels of the wind, Te Ua said, would visit the faithful during the rites. And to make it easier for the angels to descend, ropes' ends dangled from the yards, participants holding them as they circled the mast as though in a maypole dance. Engaging in the rites, Te Ua said, would make the participants invulnerable to the bullets of the white man. In battle, soldiers of the *Pai-marire* should raise the right hand, palm outwards and fingertips to wrist in the vertical plane parallel to the body, and shout '*Pai-marire-hau! hau!*'

The Maori word *hau*, uttered staccato as a bark, may refer to the wind, to breath, or the life principle. Reduplicated, and used as a verb, it has the meaning 'Strike! Attack!'[3] To the call '*Poriri-hoia!* Fall-in, Soldiers!' the congregation would gather round the pole or *niu*, take up a military order, and process round the pole. The chants were repetitive, many being

---

[1] In *Babbage* (p. 30) it is represented that this symbol is a bow and arrow, and, since the Maori did not use bows and arrows, the symbol, it is said, shows how European elements are mixed in with the traditional Maori culture. But though there is evidence that Maori knew about bows and arrows, and might have thought of this symbol as a bow and arrow, those conversant with Polynesian art styles and symbolism will know that an oft-repeated motif, especially among the Maori, was that of a tongue protruding from the mouth of a divinity, thus:

To the present writer it seems much more likely that the symbol ⊖ is a diagrammatic representation of the protruding tongue, the meanings of which cluster round the themes of generative, competent and defiant power (Cf. *Langewis*). *Harrop*, p. 160, shows the flag of the Maori King with a cruciform and three stars.

[2] *niu* in traditional Maori culture were sticks or poles used in divination rituals.

[3] The Maori word *hau* is exceedingly complex. Generally speaking it carries the idea of power being exerted. Reduplicated and used as a noun (*hauhau*) it is the bludgeon used for killing birds. See *Williams, H. W.*; *Cowan*, pp. 6–7; *Winks*, pp. 200–2; *Tregear*.

pidgin renderings of European phrases. Thus

> *To Mai Niu Kororia, mai merire!*
> *To rire, rire!*
>
> My Glorious Niu, have mercy on me!
> Have mercy, mercy![1]

would be repeated several times, the words *mai-marire* being
thought to be Maori renderings of the Latin *miserere mei*.[2] One
of the *Pai-marire* prayers translates in abbreviated form as
follows:

> By belief in the Ruler, all men shall be saved in the day of the
> passing over and the pouring out of blood, lest they should be
> touched by the destroyer, the enemy, the Governor, and his sol-
> diers. This is my earnest striving to you, O Ruler, that the heart of
> the Governor should be drawn forth by you that it may be
> withered up in the sun, not to see any brightness because he is the
> Bad Devil in the world, and destroyer of men.[3]

The 'Governor', of course, refers to the head of the white colonial
administration.

The *Pai-marire* or *Hauhau* movement first came to the notice
of the colonial government in a battle. A Captain Lloyd with a
company of soldiers penetrated into the country where Te Ua
was influential, and, posting his sentries without due care, the
captain and his men were ambushed by a party of Maori
charging down on them from the bush and shouting '*Pai-marire-
hau! hau!*' Taken by surprise, the soldiers were routed, leaving
many dead and wounded behind them. These last the Hauhaus
decapitated, smoking the heads in traditional manner and then
exhibiting them around the neighbourhood. With this initial
victory the movement spread fast. Tall *niu* poles were erected in
village after village. Te Ua instructed disciples and lieutenants
in the prayers, rites and incantations of the movement. There
were further acts of savagery. A lone missionary, a man who
had lived amongst the Maori for most of his working life, and
who had hitherto been apparently well loved by them, was
crucified, his eyes being swallowed whole as a symbol of the
treatment to be meted out to Queen and Parliament.[4] Further
miraculous powers were attributed to Te Ua. It was said, for

[1] *Cowan*, p. 10.   [2] Idem.   [3] *Harrop*, p. 244.   [4] *Harrop*, p. 247.

example, that through his own spirit familiar—in Polynesian tradition sorcerers were believed to have spirit familiars from whom they obtained information and instructions not available to ordinary men—which appeared to him in the guise of an owl, he was forewarned of, and thus escaped, a punitive expedition which had been sent out to capture him. Such incidents, whether or not they actually occurred, were thought or believed to have occurred, had wide currency, and confirmed the popular belief in Te Ua's great personal *mana* or powers and qualities of leadership and command. He was successfully doing what he said he could do.

In the face of organized European soldiery, however, a militant movement such as the *Pai-marire* could not last for long. In 1886 Te Ua surrendered to General Chute and pleaded for clemency both for himself and his followers. This clemency was granted and honoured.

That the overt and efficient impetus of the movement was based in economic conditions is hardly to be doubted. One of the chiefs of Opotoki informed Bishop Williams of his conversion to *Pai-marire* with the words:

> Bishop, many years ago we received the faith from you. Now we return it to you, for there has been found a new and precious thing by which *we shall keep our land*.[1]

Again, as one Hauhau adherent harangued a group of villagers:

> These men, these missionaries, were always telling us, 'Lay up for yourselves treasure in heaven'. And so, while we were looking up to heaven, *our land was snatched away* from beneath our feet.[2]

Land and who should use it for what was a real and concrete problem. For while the Maori system of subsistence agriculture required large parcels of land which could be allowed to return to forest, lie fallow, and then support the growth of the numerous wild stuffs which the Maori also harvested, the Europeans required relatively small areas of permanently cultivated lands, and vast areas of grassland on which they could rear sheep. The conversion of forest and scrub into permanent grassland affected the Maori most. They had no sheep and were not interested in rearing them even if they could get hold of them.

[1] *Cowan*, p. 492 (my italics).   [2] *Harrop*, p. 280 (my italics).

They were deprived of important foodstuffs, edible wild flora and fauna. They were unable to get sufficient access to traditional industrial material resources such as wood and fibrous plants.

Keeping in mind the positively expressed objectives of learning English and all the arts and sciences of Europeans, which activities represent new assumptions about power, new ways of expressing obligations, new redemptive media, it is still worthwhile pursuing the issue of land. For this was more than a valuable economic resource. Traditional Maori sentiments of attachment to particular parcels of land, on account of their association with the ancestors, social groupings and deities, joined the living with the glories and values of the past. Through the industrious and efficient exploitation and conservation of land and its resources a man gained prosperity and prestige, made himself worthy of the ancestors, commanded respect from his fellows. Further, intimately related to gaining and losing lands were the capacities to fight and wage war successfully. These features were of prime importance in the accumulation of *mana*: that power of command over resources and other people which contained the essence of Maori integrity.[1] Thus, while the loss of their lands put Maori integrity squarely in question, the *Pai-marire* not only brought together the relevances of land and war, but, in rescuing these traditional criteria of integrity for the future, also pointed to new ways in which a new and larger integrity, a more embracing redemption, might be won.

The King movement reveals the Maori as beginning to adopt the political symbols, forms, and presumably part at least of the categories of understanding of the wider and more powerful community. But this political response could not but fail. The balance of powers was too one-sided. There is little evidence of any real consensus as between Pakeha (whites) and Maori. And

---

[1] The ability to fight and wage war successfully was intimately related to virility, sexual prowess and generative powers. Genital powers, command over others, fruitful exploitation of land resources, and the ability to fight well with courage and cunning, together spelled out the requirements of integrity.

On *mana* see *Gudgeon*; *Hogbin*; *Williamson* (2); *Capell*; *Firth* (3), among many other more imaginative but perhaps less reliable analyses.

even if there was it would be naïve to think that the differences
in power deployed by either side would not have been exploited. Nevertheless, it might well be asked whether, without
the experience of the political failure of the King movement
behind them, any Maori would have rallied to Te Ua and his
Pai-marire movement. We can hazard a guess, but we cannot
know. On the other hand, we can say that since the *Pai-marire*
overleaped and transcended the political objectives of the 'King
movement', the latter may have been a necessary educative
preliminary. Moreover, we do know that the religious content
of the *Pai-marire*—those new assumptions about power the
effects of which, Te Ua asserted, would more than counter-
balance the differences in powers wielded by Pakeha and Maori
—survived the apparent political failures of the King and *Pai-
marire* movements to be realized in a quasi-political form later
on. For after the Hauhaus had been broken up, Te Kooti, once
a *Pai-marire* convert who had been captured by government
forces and deported, returned to his native village after peace
had been established. And there he founded what was to
become a dissident but syncretic religious sect known as the
Ringatau.[1] Welding together selected Christian and Maori
elements, the *Ringatau*, whose core is composed of the descend-
ents of the followers of Te Kooti, survives today.

Given this continuum between the King movement, the *Pai-
marire*, and the *Ringatau*, the 'success' or 'failure' of the *Pai-
marire* can only be very narrowly judged by reference to the
hopeless war, the mast and its ropes' ends, Te Ua begging for
clemency, or an angel slithering down a rope to make a warrior
invulnerable to bullets. Rather should it be judged by the
Ringatau on the one hand, and current conditions and assumptions in the Waikato and Taranaki areas on the other. For these
conditions of being, despite what particular individuals at the
relevant times might have thought they could foresee, want, or
bring about, are what in fact the *Pai-marire* movement helped
in an important way to effect. Whether we conceive of the time
perspective as spread over a period of weeks, years or generations, we ought to think of a millenarian movement as having
(possible) political antecedents and sectarian consequences. It
suggests, at the least, that we should look for antecedents and

[1] See *Greenwood.*

consequences, sectarian or otherwise. By looking at the sequence of events objectively we may gain some understanding of what at first sight seems silly, ill-considered, and even unrelated.

THE SIOVILI OR 'JOE GIMLET' CULT[1]

The activities known as the *Siovili* or Joe Gimlet cult—*Sio* is anglicized to 'Joe', and a *vili* is a drill or gimlet—took place in Samoa in the 'thirties and 'forties of the last century. Like other Polynesians, the Samoans were a proud and aristocratic people. They were disdainful of the first Europeans of their acquaintance, thinking them inferior, unhealthy and smelly. Still, after a few years they began to covet the varieties of artifacts which Europeans had. And they connected the possession of these goods not so much with the abilities and capacities of Europeans themselves as with their forms of belief, their assumptions about power. If by believing in entities called 'God' and 'Jesus Christ' and following a series of prescribed rituals these lesser folk could have all these goods, what was to prevent Samoans gaining the same kind of access? It was in this kind of ambience of eager and covetous expectation that Siovili, nicknamed Joe Gimlet, was to find his metier.

Siovili was a native-born Samoan, an early convert to Christianity who always thought of himself as a Christian. He had travelled widely in European ships, visiting Australia among other places. Of particular importance is the fact that one of his voyages had taken him to Tahiti where he had been closely associated with the *Mamaia* movement. This, taking place in 1827, was essentially a politically based schism between two parties of Tahitian Christians. Nevertheless, in the course of the dispute activities of millenarian type took place, and Siovili, a man who was in any case subject to trances, visions, and traditional forms of spirit possession, was much impressed.

When, soon after his Tahitian experience, Siovili returned to Samoa, he had a number of visions which, in revealing a variety of rites and practices, also held out the promise of an abundance of European goods. He attracted a number of followers, who also believed themselves to be Christians. 'Don't speak to me,'

[1] See *Freeman.*

said a Siovili adherent to a Samoan Christian teacher who had been warning him of the dangers of eternal damnation, 'I have got a foreign religion as well as you, and mine is as good as yours. Attend to your own soul, I am attending to mine.'[1] So far as one may speak of 'worship' in this context, Jehovah and Jesus Christ were worshipped by Siovili and his adherents; Jehovah and Jesus Christ were thought to be speaking through Siovili. Access to European goods seems to have been thought to go with the fact of being a Christian. But we cannot without some distortion say that Samoans became Christians in order to obtain European goods—though of course it is possible that some did. Many Samoans who wanted European goods did not become Christians.

One of Siovili's followers was an old woman, herself subject to trances and spirit possession.[2] And she, believing herself to have become possessed by Jesus Christ, announced that Christ was about to return to earth, and that the dead would rise from their graves. Growing crops, she went on, should be plucked from the ground and thrown away; cemeteries should be weeded and tidied. Then Jesus would come walking across the sea, destroy everything, and call down an abundance of food, crops and manufactured goods from the sky. The people of the woman's neighbourhood, most of whom seem to have been Christians, did as they were bid, assembling on the beach to await the coming of the Lord. The first day passed. . . . 'To-morrow,' said the old lady encouragingly, 'Tomorrow He will come.' The second day passed. . . . 'Christ wishes us to wait three days,' said the old lady. The third day came and went. After the fourth day the expectant community returned to their gardens to rescue what they could of their crops. Nonetheless, Siovili's followers retained their integrity as a group, and survived as such in Samoa for a couple of decades or more. They would gather together in lonely bush places to pray, particularly in a dark hut where lay the tattered remnants of a bible which *Siovili* claimed he had been able to read. No less than the manufactured goods of Europeans the capacity of white folk to read and write and so communicate with each

[1] *Freeman*, p. 191.
[2] As a woman, of course, she was in an under-privileged position. Cf. *Lewis* (and below, p. 161).

other over distances impressed them greatly.[1]

A hymn sung by followers of Siovili translates as follows:

> Dash did the ship of the two sailors through the waves,
>   Necklaces, O Necklaces!
> They two arrived at the country of Britain,
>   Necklaces, O Necklaces!
> A Great Lord is the King of the Skies,
>   Necklaces, O Necklaces!
> Cry to be sent, cry to be sent,
>   Necklaces, O Necklaces!
> Siovili sailed with the ship dashing through the waves,
>   Necklaces, O Necklaces!
> And the living water is come to Eva [in Samoa],
>   Necklaces, O Necklaces!
> Dash did the ship of the two sailors through the waves,
>   Necklaces, O Necklaces!
> And they two arrived at Botany Bay,
>   Necklaces, O Necklaces!
> The Governor is a great King,
>   Necklaces, O Necklaces!
> Dash did the ship of the two sailors through the waves,
>   Necklaces, O Necklaces!
> The two reached the Land of Compassion,
>   Necklaces, O Necklaces!
> A Great Lord is King Jehovah,
>   Necklaces, O Necklaces![2]

The hymn, which reveals both Christian and traditional Samoan elements, and which reflects the personal experiences of Siovili himself in the greater community, was sung in the manner of the traditional dancing songs. The chorus 'Necklaces, O Necklaces!' refers to the strings of blue beads which the first Europeans brought to Samoa, and which became the symbol of the white man's goods. In the *Pai-marire* case, it will be remembered, the Governor was an object of malediction. Here the Governor is praised. Looking at these features more closely we can perhaps appreciate that whilst many Maori were literate and had enjoyed a reasonable access to European goods by the sale of their lands, they could not stem the flood of white settlers, their objections to whom they personalized in

[1] Compare the *Pai-marire*, above, p. 16.

[2] *Freeman*, p. 188. There is no indication who the 'two sailors' were.

the Governor. In the Samoan case, where there was no settler problem, the economic component of the activities centred around access to a different kind of scarce commodity, European manufactured goods. The Governor, a remote but powerful representative of the whites, is praised and implicitly prayed to give of his bounty as a Samoan chief would be expected to do.[1] In both cases, however, the significance of the economic components is defined by their relation to prestige and integrity, not simply by virtue of scarcity or becoming scarcer.

Samoans, like other Polynesians, found prestige in *mana*— command over others—a feature which went together with a series of graduated titles. These could be earned, or retained when inherited, by a judicious and efficient use of resources in order to provide feasts and participate in exchanges of treasure articles such as fine mats and *tapa* cloth. To give the kinds of feasts which would add to his *mana* and qualify him for higher titles, to increase his turnover of exchanges of treasure articles in relation to others—which also added to *mana* and was a necessary qualification for gaining higher titles—a man had to be able to command the goodwill, co-operation and labour of others. And this he could only do, first, by demonstrating his industry, skill, efficiency and organizational powers in the basic subsistence activities, fishing and horticulture; and second, by conforming to the image of the good man—roughly, cunning, effectiveness and generosity unalloyed by greed and selfishness. Though of course the possession or lack of a variety of other attributes and qualities might add to, or detract from, these basic requirements, the latter were quite definitive. But the differential between those of otherwise apparently equal merit—for almost all in a community were more or less equally competent at fishing and farming, only the inherently lazy or mentally deficient or obstinately non-conformist being markedly inferior in productive capacity—was to be found in the rates of turnover of exchanges of treasure articles. The man with a relatively high or increasing rate of turnover attracted followers and dependants. The man with a relatively low or decreasing rate of turnover found it difficult to retain such followers and dependants as he might have had. Herein lay the value and significance of European goods: they could be exchanged.

[1] There was no 'Governor' in Samoa at the time.

Having scarcity value as well as reflecting the initiative and ability of one who could obtain them, the passage of European goods in an exchange could make all the difference in a generalized situation of competition for *mana* and titles. Even today village Samoans pursue European goods, chiefly tinned fish, not for purposes of consumption but to pass on to others in exchange. Samoans are thus involved in a credit system in which the more able gain the confidence of others. The capacity to gain such confidence indicates the meaning of *mana*, and the possession of *mana* is acknowledged in titles.

The activities associated with Siovili do not amount to much. Politically insignificant, they were simply a scatter of episodes which troubled no administration though they possibly amused the few resident Europeans. Nevertheless, they can be analysed within the terms suggested. And these identify the activities as millenarian in nature. Encountering a different kind of power, and different assumptions about power—those of Europeans—some Samoans attempted to come to terms with them. At the time politically oppressed by no one in particular, but coveting European goods, some Samoans yet felt themselves oppressed or frustrated by their inability to obtain a sufficiency of European goods. This prevented them from gaining those heights of prestige and integrity which the possession of European goods would have given them the opportunity to attain. Or, to put it another way, they had to be content with less than the best. Conceiving a higher, finer or more difficult or worthwhile mode of redemption, they had to be content with a lower, grosser and less satisfying one. With assumptions about power—particularly those whose realization could add to *mana* and so to an overall integrity—in question, a well-travelled prophet, experienced in the ways of white men and their powers, not only expressed current doubts but attempted to resolve them by articulating acceptable answers: 'Take over European assumptions about power if you want their kinds of powers.'

As in the *Pai-marire*, the 'success' or 'failure' of the activities sparked off by Siovili should not be judged against the disappointment of those who waited in vain for Christ to come over the sea, nor by the continuing normal weather conditions which failed to shower goods from the sky. These are things which we who know so much better can afford to chuckle about.

Rather should we note the sustained interest of Siovili's followers in attempting to realize the new assumptions which had been brought into their cognizance, the attention they paid to the techniques of the new powers they had encountered—writing in particular—and the conditions obtaining in the region when Siovili himself was but a memory or almost forgotten. Siovili and his followers put to the test an hypothesis about power, and in the action something was learned about the truth.

A COOK ISLANDS MOVEMENT

Both the *Pai-marire* and *Siovili* activities, which occurred over a century ago, show us small groups of people attempting to grasp at viable assumptions about the conditions of being in an environment in which power, and the allocation of particular kinds of power, were changing or had changed. Much nearer our own time, but with the same kinds of relevance, is a movement which is reported as having taken place in the Cook Islands in 1947.[1] In this case the prophet was an old lady with a reputation for powers of spirit possession. She had made a journey to Rarotonga, and whilst there two spirits had appeared to her in a dream. They told her to return home and prepare the people to receive a shipload of European goods which would come to her island in a spirit ship. Accordingly, the old lady returned to her native village, called a meeting, and was soon possessed by the spirit of her elder brother. The latter spoke through her to the assembled villagers, instructing them to make a sacred place or *marae*. When the *marae* was complete the spirit ship would come to the island laden with bully beef—at the time the most desired and scarcest imported food. Though the site indicated by the spirit as proper for the *marae* was about two miles inland, since the ship was to be a spirit ship this was no obstacle.

At some expense in voluntary labour and sweat, therefore, the *marae* was built, and the community waited as the appointed day for the ship to arrive drew nigh. At the last moment, however, the prophet insisted that her followers should receive a form of baptism—a mark on the forehead made with red clay and water in the name of Satan. One man refused this baptism.

[1] See *Crocombe*.

He asserted that he had already been baptized in Christ. At this the old lady exclaimed that now all their efforts would probably be in vain. Still, she would ask the gods to be merciful and send the ship notwithstanding. . . .

After three days of waiting for the ship at the *marae* the company disbanded, blaming the single recalcitrant for the failure of the ship to arrive.

Though this Cook Islands movement bears most of the hallmarks of a typical Melanesian 'cargo' movement, if we remember the old woman of the *Siolvili* activities,[1] the role of the *marae* in the *Pai-marire*,[2] and know something about traditional forms of spirit possession in Polynesia,[3] we can appreciate that the cultural idiom is Polynesian rather than Melanesian. It is also worth bearing in mind that the Cook Islanders were converted to Christianity in the 1820s and 1830s—five or six generations of Christians. While there is little doubt that, in common with other administrations, the administration of the Cook Islands might be improved, no one could within reason call it oppressive. Yet life tends to be dull, few ships call, the islands are isolated, aside from the mainstream of civilized and moneyed life. The inhabitants live within the confines of a simple subsistence economy based on horticulture and fishing. There are a few trading concerns which sell sundry supplies and provisions and bring a little money into the islands through the export of copra and dried sea foods. The administration itself brings money into the islands, and migrants to New Zealand send some of their wages home to their relatives. Still, some Cook Islanders, who perhaps were unable to make money for themselves, coveted the goods that only money can buy. As was the case with Siovili and his followers, the Cook Islanders in question may be taken to have conceived a different or more satisfying form of redemption. Either, with goods coming freely across the sea, they would have been discharged from all obligations of a material kind; or, given such access to goods, they would have been able to discharge their personal obligations to each other in terms of assumptions which included the power to gain free access to the goods. And with the help of a travelled old lady they attempted to realize the assumptions

[1] Above, p. 23.　　　　[2] Above, p. 17.

[2] See *Ellis*; *Best*; *Williamson* (1) and (2); *Firth* (4); *Guiart* (3).

she had articulated to them. She it was who seemed to bring the improbable into the field of the possible.

How difficult was it for the old lady to do this?

Not all millenarian movements evidence the spirituality some might prefer as the basis of religious activity. If true faith springs only from syntheses of spiritual and pragmatic experience, we welcome the confident assurance that life would be just as we wanted it to be if we but filled in the coupon. Though for many Europeans of an idealist or romantic turn of mind the Polynesian Islands seem a paradise where no one need worry about money, for some Polynesians it is perhaps this very lack of money that contributes towards envisaging a millennium where there is an abundance of those things that only money can buy.

4

Matters Arising

The three examples from Polynesia have shown how the inter-dependence between assumptions about power, redemption, and integrity—whether this last is expressed in relation to land, access to goods, or money—can be drawn from the historical narrative. We have also seen how millenarian activities may be preceded by a political movement or accommodation and succeeded by sectarian religious activity; in what sense the 'success' or 'failure' of a particular set of millenarian activities should be judged not within terms of the activities themselves but within their context of a time perspective that includes both antecedents and later developments; and that effective prophets may be women as well as men. We may now go on to consider some other matters that arise from the examples.

CULTURAL IDIOM

Some of the resemblances in the examples above may be summed up as a 'cultural idiom'. This refers to particular ways of engaging in millenarian activities which, though consistent with the more abstract and general pattern, may be peculiar to the culture concerned. If a prophet is to communicate, be accepted and recognized, he has to say and do things which are familiar and intelligible to his audience, and which will impress them. In the *Pai-marire* movement flags, a St. George's cross and a cruciform or St. Andrew's cross demonstrate the attempt to adopt, and so come to terms with, Europeans and Christians and their ideas and assumptions: the idiom is European or Christian. The flag inscribed with a ꝑ represents a synthesis: for a flag is a European symbol of power, and the inscription seems to be a traditional Maori symbol of power.[1] The ship's

---

[1] Above, p. 17, n. 1.

mast was erected as a flagpole, a European sign of resident authority. But it was called a *niu*, and *niu* are traditionally divination sticks used as an aid to coming to an action decision where the balance of forces in a situation is equivocal, or not wholly predictable from experience. Te Ua himself was Maori-cum-Christian. On the one hand he had a spirit familiar which took the form of an owl—a quite usual circumstance with traditional Maori seers, visionaries, sorcerers and those subject to trances—and on the other hand he was versed in the scriptures and had visions of the angel Gabriel, a Christian representation of power.

Women in Polynesia quite frequently have trances and spirit familiars. In themselves the experiences of the two female prophets would conform to traditional cultural expectations. But the content and consequences of their experiences involved a marriage between traditional and Christian or European representations and assumptions about power. Siovili's hymn was sung to traditional Samoan rhythms and tunes. But its words opened a prospect not limited by purely traditional Samoan horizons. On the other hand, though not wholly unknown in Polynesian tradition, the Cook Islander's spirit communication with a dead elder brother is much more typical of Melanesia than Polynesia; and so is the expression of the millennium in terms of the arrival of a quantity of European goods.

It is possible that, since the old lady of the Cook Islands had travelled, she had heard about Melanesian cargo cults, and that this knowledge influenced her experiences and revelation. But the point here is not to pose the problem of tracing out the possible origins of a particular revelation, but rather to draw attention to the fact that while millenarian activities may be expressed in a variety of idioms, it is our job to elicit those common principles or sets of logical relations indicated by the differing idioms. We know that among ourselves millenarian movements have had a common basis in Christian traditions, that particular expressions or idioms vary with historical period and circumstances and with national or regional boundaries. In the same way prophets in other lands take departure from their own local or greater traditions. However strange or bizarre the new aspirations may seem to a foreigner, to be communicable to the indigenous audience they must be cast in a traditional mould. Both in this and a deeper sense all prophets take on themselves the task of renovating tradition, of seeking into the familiar and accepted in order to reach forward into the new, of so phrasing the new that it emerges as a more appropriate expression of what had always been agreed to be true. Nevertheless, in the attempt to rediscover and remould the traditional sources of authority and power, a prophet, by digging new channels for tradition, also allows the new to flow in.[1] And only through a close acquaintance with the relevant cultural idioms does it become possible to appreciate the styles in which particular prophets fulfil themselves and make explicit what their audiences feel, but cannot effectively say, they want.

INCIDENCE

The question of cultural idiom leads directly to the incidence of millenarian movements. Are some cultures more prone to these activities than others, and if so why? The largest number of recorded instances are surely to be found in Europe, and in European developments overseas.[2] Whether this is because of Christian traditions of millenarism, or because of the peculiar fondness of Europeans for chronicling and recording, are questions which we cannot yet answer. While there is evidence to suggest that the tribes of Europe had much the same troubles with the Romans as divers peoples have had with European colonial endeavours,[3] European traditions of millenarism have to be traced back through the pentecostal tradition set by the apostles to the ancient Hebrews and thence to the first civilizations in the fertile crescent in the middle east.[4] Yet the Islamic world, which shares with Christianity its older traditions, yields relatively few examples.[5] And although Islam certainly allows for the emergence of further prophets, the acute political sense of

[1] Cf. *Scholem*, pp. 7–14.

[2] The difficulties of making an accurate count are well-nigh unsurmountable. But a glance through the literature leaves no doubt that the vast bulk of millenarian activities are European in origin.

[3] For some examples see *Owen*.

[4] See *Wallis*.

[5] The Mahdi and El Bab movements are perhaps the best known. (*Fulop-Miller*, pp. 80–100; *Browne*.)

Mohammed and his immediate successors, the very firm political control exercised in Islamic countries in the past, and Sunni iconoclasm and distaste for the emotional excesses so often associated with millenarian activities, go some way towards accounting for the relative dearth. Outside the ambience of Christian missionary work in India, China, central Asia, Japan, and South-east Asia—an area containing the large bulk of the world's population—we find even fewer instances. Still, we may count as generally millenarian the activities associated with Gautama Buddha, Mahavira the first Jain, Kabir, Shih Huang Ti, Ghengis Khan, Tamerlane, and Jimmu Ten.[1]

Examples from Latin or South American aboriginal peoples are beginning to mount, and so are those from Africa.[2] In North America the Eskimos seem to have remained immune until, with the economic depression of the 'thirties which ruined the fur trade on which they had almost entirely depended, some groups decided to mould their lives anew.[3] And much the same sudden economic exigencies seem to have played a large part in the few examples we have from the north-west coast.[4] The Plains Indians, on the other hand, provide us with several examples.[5] Strong in their own traditions, but competing against pioneers and an army with an industrialized backing, the Plains Indians engaged in millenarian activities only when their culture had been virtually destroyed. Confronted with the fact of physical defeat, they had to search for new assumptions. The Pueblo Indians of the south-west provide a number of minor instances.[6] Influenced by Europeans and their ideas, but rarely competing with them for the same resources, the Pueblo activities reveal for the most part a generally studied absorption of new things and ideas. When we turn to the Oceanic material

[1] On Gautama see *Brewster*; *Thomas*. On Mahavira see *Stevenson*; *Jaini*. On Kabir see *MacAuliffe*. On Shih Huang Ti see *Fitzgerald* (1) and (2). On Ghengis Khan see *Lamb* (1). On Tamerlane see Lamb (2). On Jimmu Ten see *Sansom*; *Sadler*.

[2] For examples from Africa see *Sundkler, Balandier,* and for examples from South America see *Queiroz, Butt.*

[3] *Mathiassen*, p. 235; *Honigmann*, pp. 69–71.

[4] See for examples, *Barnett*; *Gunther*; *Smith* (1).

[5] See for examples *Hoebel* (1); *Lesser*; *Mooney.*

[6] See for examples *Hill*; *Dozier*, pp. 122–62; and implications in *Burridge* (4).

we find that recorded instances in Polynesia and Micronesia have been comparatively rare: up to forty occurrences, say, over a period of a century and a half. Among Australian aborigines only two or three instances emerge, and these are very recent. But in the islands of Melanesia recorded examples run into their hundreds over a period of rather less than a century.

While it is not possible to account in detail in the space of this essay for these apparent disparities of incidence, we can make some tentative suggestions. The remarks made in passing, above, that a powerful political regime, iconoclasm, a robust adherence to traditional ways, and the lack of a competitive situation could account, severally, for a relative dearth of instances seem logically to hold. To a powerful and ruthless political regime millenarian activities are anathema. They question that which may not be questioned: the sources and allocations of particular kinds of power. Consequently, incipient activities and movements are usually entirely suppressed, the participants being imprisoned or executed as an example to others. If one asks about the case of a powerful but tolerant regime, the reply is that if this is not a contradiction in terms it is an irrelevant question. A powerful regime is a powerful regime. It can choose to ignore a little harmless excitement, it can also choose to obliterate it. As we shall see in more detail, the most favourable political conditions for the emergence of a millenarian movement seem to be when tolerance is a euphemism for the kind of regime which is either not powerful enough to suppress the activities, or which for a variety of reasons is inhibited from deploying the power at its disposal. This fits the European and European colonial situations—which contain the vast bulk of recorded millenarian activities.

Iconoclasm and a robust adherence to traditional ways are two facets of the same attitude: no adulteration of the pure tradition. And if we are right in thinking that millenarian activities envisage new ways, then it is clear that, depending on the strength of these two qualities, a people deeply committed to a particular tradition will be inhibited from engaging millenarian activities. Finally, competition is surely implicit in all that has been said. Millenarian activities arise from a competitive situation. They constitute a challenge to accepted or current conditions and assumptions, invite suppression by a powerful regime, and occur where the regime, though powerful, is inhibited. A regime confirmed in its traditional forms and ways, and which will not brook alternatives, provides unfavourable conditions.

That the vast bulk of recorded instances of millenarian activity should have taken place within Judaeo-Christian traditions, or where Christians, missionaries or otherwise, have had significant influence, is certainly of great importance.[1] But though there is a sense in which we cannot do other than define a millenarian movement in terms of our own Judaeo-Christian traditions, we have to allow that activities of a millenarian kind can occur without the specific intervention of Christianity. Granted that Christianity is a millenarian faith with a particular style and content, we stand upon firmer ground if we look more closely not so much at Christianity in itself as at the day-to-day exercise of assumptions about power: operations on the political stage. For we have one example of millenarian type activities that took place among a New Guinea people when they sighted an aircraft—this before they had seen or heard of Christians, Europeans, or any other sophisticated people.[2] And what these New Guineans saw, surely, was a deployment and demonstration of capacities and power which they had to absorb and explain to themselves if they were to continue to retain their integrity as men. Aware of themselves in the terms of one set of assumptions, they had now to become aware of themselves in terms of assumptions that included something more. A new kind of redemption was offered, and to take advantage of this a certain reorganizing of political relations seems to have been entailed.

Suggesting logical reasons why millenarian movements should not occur is one matter. But to explain why they should occur, or why they should not occur among a particular people whose neighbours are being actively millenarian, are more

[1] Christian missionaries have always and traditionally been the friends of the poor and helpless. Long before anthropologists or sociologists arrived on the scene they were there, teaching a new way of life, protecting their charges from rapacious traders, championing their causes in the face of administrations which were often obtuse.

[2] *Berndt* (2).

difficult problems. Despite the time perspective within which a
movement or set of activities should be judged if their impact
on, and relevance to, the developing social order are to be more
thoroughly understood, each movement or set of activities must
be regarded as existentially self-justifying. An outsider may take
it upon himself to say that a particular movement is due to
these kinds of economic circumstance, or those kinds of
deprivation. Yet in the end we are left with a series of economic
circumstances and kinds of deprivation. On examining other
situations with the same kinds of economic circumstances and
deprivation we find that no millenarian movements have taken
place. The point is not that the negative instance is always the
more difficult to account for, or that it necessarily needs
accounting for. Rather is it that if we were to take any random
selection of individuals and group them together as a community we would soon begin to find economic hardships and
deprivations. But would there be a millenarian movement? Unless we can answer this question positively, not only are
millenarian movements self-justifying to the participants but
they must be regarded as such in an objective sense, as things in
themselves. Only by so doing may we move from possible
through probable to necessary concomitants.

The assumption that millenarian activities are somehow
troublesome and avoidable; that with a more enlightened
administration they would not occur; that it is in men's hands
to prevent them occurring without having to suppress them—
these attitudes lead into an impasse of competing intellectual
and ideological millenarisms. Pioneers, settlers, missionaries,
traders and administrators, themselves impelled by their own
millennial aspirations, know that they can make other peoples'
lands yield more bountiful harvests. That millenarian activities
were and are unavoidable surely provides a more reliable point
of departure. Were we to attempt to make them occur—would
we not come nearer to understanding why they do occur? If we
do the next best thing and try to stand on the believer's ground,
accept the revelation, the prophet, and the associated rites and
activities as guaranteeing the truth of things, and then attempt
to find out what kinds of truth they reveal, we may advance
our understanding of the kinds of truth that are revealed. For
on this there should be no mistake: every millenarian move-

ment carries for its participants the guarantee of divine revelation, the guarantee of creative truth itself. That we may reserve
judgement on whether the revelation seems to us 'true', 'good',
'false', or 'inefficient' is of little moment. What matters is that
in distancing ourselves from the immediate scene, and then
attempting to interrelate the 'truths' we believe we have
grasped, we are in a position to grope for truths that are wider
and deeper than those revealed either by the movement or by our
own initial assumptions. Prepared to qualify our own assumptions about power and the way life should be lived, and allowing that a revelation is divinely inspired, we can try to indicate
the kinds of situation in which the divine injunction seems to
work best.

THE POLYNESIAN SCENE IN CONTEXT

Almost everywhere in Polynesia the earlier European explorers,
traders and missionaries seem to have encountered the symptoms of a dying culture: murder, feud and warfare seemed
uncontrollable; law-keeping mechanisms seemed to be degenera-
ting. The scene was one of incipient anomy. How much this was
due to sighting Europeans and their goods,[1] the largesse of men
like Cook and Bougainville, or the depredations of early whalers
and traders, is impossible to assess. But the fact remains. It was
not for nothing that, after initial recalcitrances, conversions to
Christianity were wholesale and general. In an orgy of destruction the islanders themselves razed their temples, smashed their
sacred structures and images. The new life, whatever it might
turn out to be, was greeted and espoused as better than the old.
But nowhere was the ordering of traditional familial as opposed
to political relations seriously disrupted. Land and settler
problems were confined to New Zealand. As Polynesians cast
aside the trappings and ceremonial of much of their traditional
ritual and political life, and began to explore the intricacies of
Christianity, ordinary day-to-day social life continued much as
it had done. Christianity could not but be translated into, and
seen in terms of, traditional categories of understanding. Rather
dull and colourless in comparison with the old way of life it may
have been, yet most of the requirements of an ordered social life

[1] See above, p. 35, on the sighting of an aeroplane.

seem to have been satisfied. European missionaries became petty
chiefs who demanded little more than overt sexual morality,
industry, church going and hymn singing. Reacting perhaps
from the excesses of the preceding anomies, from the lawlessness, quarrels and fighting, energies tended to spend themselves
in the quieter reaches of social life.

On the whole, with opportunities for numerous encounters
with different Europeans limited by the dispersed nature of the
island groups, those relatively few Europeans whom the indigenous communities saw frequently were well known and
understood. And they themselves had begun to appreciate the
indigenous communities. But in those places where the representatives of the two kinds of social order continually encountered each other and were pushed into competitive roles, as in
New Zealand, there we find chiliasms. Where there seemed to be
a quite unfair and arbitrary or capricious access to the goods of
the new environment, there too we find the stirrings of messianic
or millenarian activities. And common to both situations is the
fact that, given the differences inherent in the two social orders,
neither issue was susceptible to a qualitative decision acceptable
to both parties. The man with a greater access to money, however poor his other qualities and capacities, had the edge on one
who lacked this capacity or opportunity but had other qualities
in abundance. The social order with wider categories of understanding and with a privileged access to money, and so to the
goods that only money could buy, was bound to prevail over a
social order without access to money. Discrepant powers and
privileges were inherent in the circumstances.

The first white settlers in New Zealand admired the Maori and
their way of life, appreciated them, relied on them, traded and
intermarried with them. Later settlers (not without reason, for
the savagery of Maori warfare appalled Europeans of finer
susceptibilities[1]) regarded the Maori as rather lesser beings in
the scale of evolution and refused to treat with them as they

[1] The Maori were always warlike. But they found they could trade
smoked heads for muskets. And with muskets they could wage war more
effectively and so get more smoked heads to get money to buy more
muskets to wage war even more effectively. The smoked heads, in turn,
found a ready sale in Europe and America among curio hunters and
scientific cognoscenti.

did among themselves. The *Pai-marire* movement should be seen against this perhaps inevitable abuse of human dignities. For though invulnerability to bullets might seem to Europeans a silly incursion into fantasy, it also symbolized, and was a protest against, the fact that a man of quality and courage had no alternative but to die or bow the head before any kind of man with access to a gun. After years of intermittent warfare during which each was forced to appreciate the qualities of the other, Maori and Pakeha regained a mutual respect. Yet the capacity to earn and handle money within the terms of certain prescriptions, and an appreciation of the social concomitants of using money, still tends to divide them. In other parts of Polynesia, there being no settler problems, the respect of Europeans for Polynesians was only heightened by the opinions of men like Captain Cook, de Bougainville, Rousseau, Gaugin and Stevenson. But the ability to appreciate a purely quantitative system and its social concomitants, and gain access to and handle its concrete referent, money, still distinguishes the condition of one from the condition of the other, and cannot but affect the qualities of respect each might prefer to have for the other.

Let us broaden the context by looking westwards. When Europeans first came to Australia, the native peoples were either simply pushed out of the way, or they died of disease or heartbreak. But once the areas suitable for European settlement had become roughly established, the surviving peoples of the deserts and tropical forests could carry on their traditional lives almost unhindered.[1] What is remarkable about Australian aborigines is that by and large, and with the exception only of particular individuals, tribes have either continued in their traditional ways, or they have perished in the attempt to do so. Whether or not a real choice to do one or the other actually existed is not a useful question here. What matters is their sturdy commitment to their own traditions. Where they could not succeed in this aim they died, or broke up and scattered and then died. Until very recently,[2] at no point in their history do coherently organized groups of Australian aborigines seem to

[1] Over the past fifteen years or so few aborigines have not chosen to settle down at a government or mission station.

[2] *Berndt* (3); *Lommel*; *Berndt* (1).

have made the attempt to come to terms with European traditions. Now, however, as Europeans have begun to spread across the traditional preserves of the aborigines, and as aborigines have begun to abandon their traditional nomadic life, millenarian activities have started. Money is coming into aboriginal hands and the two peoples are beginning to compete. In earlier days, it is clear, the balance of power was so one-sided that competition was hardly possible. Contempt was mutual. If white Australians saw little but 'Bungs', black Australians had a similar disdain for the white men's ways. Except *ad hoc*, to buy a shirt or some such thing whilst working for or with Europeans, for example, money and the goods it could buy were of no importance to people who lived by hunting and gathering, who were deeply committed to their traditional ways. Now, however, money and goods are wanted, and so are jobs and political responsibility within the wider community.

Shifting our gaze northward with the same considerations in mind, the Melanesian experience provides some instructive contrasts. For where Polynesians had highly sophisticated hierarchical political systems and religious organizations and ideas, and Australians had rudimentary political systems but developed and complex religious notions, Melanesians with their mainly democratic and egalitarian political systems tended to be prudish, obsessional, suspicious, and much given to wrestling with their consciences.[1] Notoriously hard-headed and pragmatic, addicted to business and trading, the rather piecemeal and opportunist religious ideas of the Melanesians may be set against the more solidly founded and systematic spiritual life of Australians and Polynesians. Yet Polynesia and Australia account for very few millenarian movements. It is among the hard-headed business pragmatists of Melanesia that we find not only the large bulk of Oceanic examples, but also the most bizarre.

If we allow that democratic egalitarianism invites competition, breeding a robust self-esteem which does not give another man best until he proves it, we have to add that (aside from the missionaries perhaps) Europeans in the area—themselves extremely self-reliant and egalitarian in outlook among their own—have for the most part regarded the black-skinned

[1] See *Lawrence and Meggitt*.

Melanesians as an inferior people. Nevertheless, when like meets like competition becomes the fiercer, and in Melanesia goods and money swiftly became the common prizes of black and white alike. For Melanesians, as in Samoa,[1] European goods were wanted partly for purposes of trade and enjoyment within their own native prestige systems, but also in order to compete with Europeans on even terms. Only the deployment of goods and money could give them that prestige which was recognizably most worthwhile, and which was clearly greater than that to which they could attain in their own communities. But the possibility of achieving this end has been largely unrealizable. Many Melanesians have become Christians, but money, access to which would enable them to engage in a redemptive process on equal terms with Europeans, has inevitably eluded them. That the moral exclusion was, and often still is, quite mutual despite the similarities in outlook, underlines the importance of money and the different conditions of being its presence or absence implies.

MONEY

Millenarian activities, we have suggested, indicate competing sets of assumptions which, in turn, point to competing moral systems or social orders. Too much power on one side, however, makes competition impossible. While there may be attempts at millenarian activity, if the more powerful group actually exerts its power the development of millenarian thoughts into activities tends to be inhibited or snubbed out altogether. On the other hand, when the competing moral systems have some common ground in certain vital assumptions, then a millenarian movement is likely. Or, to put it in another way, millenarian activities are likely where, sharing or wanting to share a common set of assumptions which point to a particular redemptive process, one of the groups concerned is debarred from access to the rewards of the assumptions and cannot earn the kind of redemption implied. Female prophets are usefully appreciated in this light. For besides being prophets in the ordinary sense they also participate in an infrastructure of competition and privilege, that of men versus women in a world where men are

[1] Above, pp. 25–6.

privileged.[1] Given this particular kind of competitive ambience, the relevant point of contact—through which we are enabled to recognize the existence of competing moral systems—lies in our ability to distinguish different ways of measuring the man, different kinds of redemptive process. In this the presence or absence of money is vital. Money goes along with particular moral and social relations.

Making a radical distinction between social orders which use money as a basic measure of man, and those which do not, is crucial.[2] In the first case, a 'complex economy', we have a highly differentiated division of labour; money; free exchange of goods and services through money and markets; generalized full-time specialization; conservation of wealth through the generations; and a basic measure of prestige and status by reference to money, though of course a variety of other qualities and capacities also enter the situation. In the second case, a 'subsistence economy', we have a simple division of labour, a set of relations in which the tasks to be performed are basically determined by age and sex; a prescribed and specific use of treasure articles; specific and prescribed types of exchange; no money; part-time specialization; and a basic measure of prestige and status by reference to the subsistence activities which most or all undertake in common—though again, a variety of other capacities also enter into the situation. It is true that in some subsistence communities there are one or two magical, ritual, or even technological full-time specialists. But where these exist they are almost always found to have a prestige of their own; they are insulated from the requirements of the main prestige system. Further, while there are numerous examples of cash circulating in subsistence economies, whether or not this money has succeeded in becoming a basic measure of prestige and status is precisely the issue. We are not comparing standards of living, for many subsistence communities are richer and have higher standards of living than particular parts of a complex economy. We are distinguishing between two sets of social

[1] Cf. *de Beauvoir*, pp. 1–128; *Lewis*; and below, p. 161.

[2] There is of course a vast literature on this question. Some authors opt for the usefulness of such a distinction, others to the contrary. See in particular: *Croome*; *Crowther*; *Dalton* (1) and (2); *Davenport*; *Einzig*; *Firth* (1), (2), (6); *Godelier*; *Steiner*, among many others.

relations which seem, in principle, to be mutually exclusive. We are drawing the divide between one kind of moral system and another.

In any community the basic measure of prestige and status must refer either to the activities which all or most undertake in common, or to those assets to which all or most in the community have a common access, or both. In addition to these basic measures other more specific qualities and capacities are usually taken into account. In a subsistence community relative abilities in the main subsistence activities emerge as the basic measures. The possession, exchange and relative turnover of treasure articles reflect or measure industry, efficiency, cunning, shrewdness, foresight and a number of other qualities; further prestige may be gained or lost by the demonstration of virtues and vices—such as virility, courage, warrior capacities, envy, secretiveness—which may be, but are not necessarily, directly related to capacities in the subsistence activities. In the complex economy, on the other hand, where with a highly differentiated division of labour there can be no one set of activities engaged in common, the basic criterion for measuring farmer, smith, carpenter, wheelright, teacher and others against each other must be that to which all have access, and by virtue of which they are enabled to specialize: money. And though one or more of a series of highly differentiated qualities and capacities are also usually taken into account, money remains the basic measure.

Succeeding to a large extent in measuring locally preferred and selected moral qualities, the treasure articles of a subsistence economy are, however, only wealth in themselves so far as, indicating particular qualities and capacities, they can be used to gain credit. For in order to get meaningful possession of such an article a man has to have been seen to do well, and in the prescribed way, the work that is required of him. Money may, but does not necessarily measure the moral qualities. It keeps, may be banked for future use, *is* wealth in a way that the treasure articles of a subsistence economy are not. For whether gotten inside or outside the law, by good or evil acts, preferred or condemned kinds of procedures, money in a complex economy can command or buy labour, things, hearts, souls and even credit. As concrete as any could wish, susceptible to touch and handling, pieces of money yet refer to an entirely abstract system of quantitative and factorial relations which endure and remain what they are through all sorts of social vicissitudes. Banks, and the keeping qualities of money, owe their permanence more to the mathematical system to which they refer than to their material construction. Whereas the relative values of treasure articles depend on intrinsic qualities as well as social and historical associations, unless an old shilling is to become a treasure article it is worth as many pennies as a new one. More subtly, money is a factorial measure of man which entails quantifying his different capacities. It separates and differentiates qualities and capacities, and in doing so gives each a referent on a quantitative scale. Further, the handling of money is an exercise in unitary and factorial relations. But qualities can only be identified within a system of binary opposites (good/bad, strong/weak, skilled/unskilled, etc.); and the factorial nature of money introduces a hierarchy of quantitative values none of which can be said to have an opposite. The two schemes, binary opposites on the one hand, and what we may call the one-and-the-many on the other, are in principle mutually opposed.

A corresponding antithesis is encountered where the worth and stature of man are measured by money and clearly differentiated capacities on the one hand, and the quality of his performance in an agglutinated 'package deal' of prescribed activities on the other. The problem is how to reconcile the antitheses. Though in practice the moneyed communities of a complex economy also use qualitative criteria, and most subsistence communities use some kind of quantitative criteria, far from detracting from the point at issue the antithesis is emphasized. A cursory glance at the millenarian activities which have taken place within the traditions of the great moneyed economies show that they turn significantly on money: on how access to money, and the uses to which money may be put, may be so prescribed and defined that this factorial and quantitative measure can accurately assess selected moral qualities. The poor man whose skills and honesty go unrecognized is as wretched as the richer whose acumen and thrift earn him nothing. Often obscured in the colonial situation by the more idealistic and humane relevances of different kinds of paternalism, this issue of quantifying and differentiating the qualities by reference to money is often ignored. Minted by the complex economy, by peoples who organize themselves into large, loose and highly differentiated entities, who engage in a multitude of specialized tasks and occupations, whose prestige systems, forms of organization and division of labour depend upon money, money quite naturally chases the stuffs its makers want, finds its way back into the pockets of those who know how to use it and make it work to advantage.

Despite attempts on the parts of colonial administrations to get money circulating amongst an indigenous people, they have always found difficulties in penetrating an indigenous prestige system based upon qualitative criteria, and then adapting or converting it to one based upon money. The indigenous qualitative criteria tend to persist. Prestige continues to depend upon competence in the subsistence activities, on turnover of exchanges, on the passage and exchange of treasure articles. The returned labourer with money in his pocket may enjoy a brief notoriety but, without a continuing access to money must needs put his hand to crook, goad, mattock, axe or adze. Such money as he may have tends to be buried, hoarded, used in *ad hoc* payments or as treasure articles.

If money is to circulate significantly, if an indigenous community is to have a satisfactory access to money, then the community must so adapt and alter its prestige system that money becomes a basic measure of worth. Unless and until money begins accurately to assess those qualities which a people or community finds meaningful, so long will they not be able to use money as it was meant to be used, so long will they not have a satisfactory access. Belonging to, and connoting, the complex social order of those who have minted it, use it, and bring it to foreign shores, money, particularly when of the more valuable or powerful currencies, demands acceptance of the kind of social ordering adopted by those who make it. Nevertheless, corrupted by a covetousness that is human, lured on by what seems to be a finer or more satisfactory means of realizing their potential, yet reluctant to abandon what tradition has hallowed, the dilemma is how to replace a current prestige system by another; how to further differentiate, factorialize and quantify the qualities; how to redefine the qualities so that they may be more satisfactorily quantified and differentiated. And both for those in a subsistence economy who want to make money a relevant measure of man, as well as for like-minded individuals within a complex economy who want to make money more accurately define the moral qualities, a millenarian movement is one way of resolving the dilemma.

To become it is first necessary to belong; and belonging makes it possible to define just who or what one is. Whether for participants or bystanders, millenarian activities provide the opportunity for becoming someone distinctive and worthwhile. And, because attitudes to money can so readily find out the man, define what is meant by integrity, millennial aspirations often find their focus in money.

5
Some Melanesian Examples

Before expanding the central issues by referring to some Melanesian instances of millenarian activity, we may signpost the ground covered thus far by a brief summary which, in its phrasing, also takes us forward into fields yet to be considered in detail. In—

    (i) taking departure from a broader meaning of 'religion' and 'religious activity' than is usual by viewing the former as a set of assumptions about power which bore upon a particular redemptive process we have seen how—

    (ii) millenarian activities, connoting the adoption of new assumptions and so a new kind of redemption, imply the making of a new culture or community.

By looking at features of cultural idiom we were able to indicate that—

    (iii) a prophet delves into tradition for his initial sources of authority, provides new channels for tradition, and fills out these new channels with new assumptions, new rules.

Though it was felt that a millenarian movement should be regarded within a time perspective that included antecedents and consequences, the general incidence of such activities suggested that—

    (iv) a millenarian movement was within itself self-justifying,

    (v) millenarian movements were inhibited either by a powerful political regime willing to use its power, or by a particularly tenacious adherence to tradition.

On the other hand, whether or not a particular tradition, such as the Christian, seemed to lend itself to recurring millenarian movements, it was—

    (vi) the tolerant political regime which seemed to provide

the conditions within which millenarian activities might prosper.

Of importance in this context was—

(vii) the competitive nature of different sets of assumptions, which could be broken down into—

(viii) competing prestige systems, characterized either by a common involvement in the self-same assumptions together with a relatively privileged access to the rewards and benefits of the assumptions on the one hand, and a relatively under-privileged access on the other; or by the inherent opposition contained in qualitative and quantitative measures of man.

Briefly indicating some Oceanic measurements of man, we selected—

(ix) money, a set of mathematical, factorial relations with concrete referents which are not convertible into a binary system of opposed qualities, as being a decisive feature.

Finally, still looking at the Oceanic scene, it seemed that—

(x) Melanesians, notoriously hard-headed business men and pragmatists, were those who were most susceptible to millenarian activities.

Melanesian millenarian activities are generally described in the literature as 'cargo' cults because, as in the Cook Islands movement described above,[1] the overtly expressed objectives of the activities are free access to European goods or cargo. The prophet (either explicitly or implicitly) promises an end to work and the advent of the millennium in terms of the arrival of quantities of European goods conditional on carrying out a variety of rites and activities. Usually the goods do not arrive. At other times, however, they do arrive. Thus when, as an act of faith in the coming millennium, a community has destroyed its crops and means of livelihood, a desperate administration often comes to the rescue, delivering sacks and cases of flour, rice, canned goods, seed crops, fertilizer and tools quite free.[2] In either event the movements recur. They continue today, and have been occurring in much the same way for nearly as century.

[1] Above, pp. 27–9.
[2] For example, in the 'Vailala Madness': *Williams, F. E.* (1) and (3).

Clearly, Melanesians want cargo. But we must surely look further than the overt ends of obtaining manufactured goods. Of course Melanesians would like a free access to European goods—Who would not? But, as has been pointed out, Melanesians are renownedly and rightly known as hard-headed and pragmatic. Traditionally reconciled to the necessity for hard work, and making a virtue out of it, Melanesians are also experts in the intricacies of trade, exchange and commerce. Relative prestige within a community depends on the public demonstration of hard work and competence in these activities. Habitually self-reliant and contemptuous of the beggar or sponger, Melanesians consider driving a hard bargain one of the prime virtues. No Melanesian is unaware that an advantage must be hard won if it is to mean anything and all are highly suspicious of what purports to be a free gift. Why then should they think that manufactured goods will come to them out of the sky, or across the sea, free?

Even if Melanesian participants in millenarian activities say that they expect cargo to arrive, and believe with the faith that moves mountains that it will arrive, it is surely more pertinent to ask what cargo means to them, what—at a deeper and symbolic level—they are seeking when attempting a free access to cargo. Not only is this kind of question analytically more useful—for who can tell what another really believes?—but it places the investigation squarely on the level of the collective. The fact that free access to cargo represents a precisely opposite condition to that presently being experienced should warn us that we are dealing with the symbolic. Perhaps free access to cargo represents the hardest kind of bargain. At any rate, we should be prepared for a synthesis between free access and difficult or no access. We should bear in mind that symbols may activate below the level of the conscious and articulate. Accepting these points, we should be able to find out what kinds of patterns of social relations enable a variety of individuals to give slightly differing reasons for wanting free access to cargo.

THE TUKA MOVEMENT, 1885

One of the earliest millenarian movements to be recorded in

Melanesia was the *Tuka* cult which took place in Fiji in 1885.[1]
There had already been signs of unrest and disaffection with
European traders and missionaries in the area concerned when,
in 1882, a man named Ndungumoi, who had travelled more than
most and who had had some acquaintance with white folk and
their ways, returned to his native village in up-country Fiji. He
claimed that he had had some marvellous adventures while he
had been away. He had been able to leave his body and return
to it, he had gained possession of charms which would render a
person invulnerable. Such claims could not but draw and hold
attention. Ndungumoi became a prophet. He assumed the title
of Navosavakandua, or Chief Justice, and announced that it
had been revealed to him that before long the whole world
would be turned upside down. The white people would serve the
Fijians, chiefs would serve commoners. Those who followed him
and took the waters of the 'fountain of life' would enjoy eternal
life. Consignments of cloth, tinned goods and other kinds of
European supplies would come in plenty. Those who disputed
his leadership, or who did not believe, would have none of these
rewards but would, on the contrary, have to serve the believers
or be condemned to hell fire.

The idea of 'reversals' is common, and many Melanesian
myths of origin place the beginnings of mankind in an earth-
quake, the reversal of a previous mode of being, or in the cosmos
turning over so that the sky, now above, was once below, and
men, once free-movers in the above, are now below, earthbound
in obligation, under instead of above the sky. Prepared for a
synthesis between these opposed conditions of being, we can see
also that the prophet used a traditional cultural idiom referring
to the origins of things. By reversing the present social order
and placing himself at the head of a new elite which would take
the place of and become like the European elite, he effected a
synthesis. He brought in new rules and assumptions as he
rechanneled a traditional source of authority.

The paradise of Ndungumoi's followers, who had to pay ten
shillings or one pound in cash for a bottle of water from the
'fountain of life', seems to have been equated with the Christian
heaven. Similarly, the sufferings of the unbelievers seems to
have been derived from Christian teaching on hell. Further,

[1] *Brewster.*

taking advantage of the apparent similarities between some Bible stories and traditional sacred myths, Ndungumoi related Genesis to the native myth of origin and, giving it a ·characteristic twist, asserted that white men had changed the names of the deities in the Genesis story. By this fraud, he went on, Europeans were claiming the Bible as their own when in reality this very important source of authority belonged to the Fijians. Consequently, Europeans were gaining access to the goods created by the divinities who all along had intended them for the Fijians. Though there seem to have been some doubts about which of the native deities or heroes should be identified with which divinities in the Bible, Ndungumoi did not permit any internal doctrinal squabbles. He assumed full authority. He extracted a membership fee from believers, and used this revenue and the cash obtained from the sale of water from the 'fountain of life' to buy foodstuffs in order to give feasts. And giving feasts was the means through which prestige was traditionally derived. He became well known in the region and people looked up to him as a man of stature. He organized his movement along paramilitary lines, by forming his followers into bands which were drilled, European fashion, by ex-policemen, and he demanded that military salutes be given him.

The climax of the movement came when, having set a date for the advent of the millennium and exhorted his followers to abandon fields and crops, he began to issue threats to Europeans. To this the administration, having both the power and the will to use it, reacted firmly. Ndungumoi and his chief disciples were rounded up and taken away to gaol. Not wanting to turn their captured prophet into a martyr or hero, however, instead of sentencing him to death the administration contented themselves with giving Ndungumoi one year's hard labour. Still, Ndungumoi's followers interpreted the mild sentence as a proof of their prophet's claim to invulnerability, and continued to believe in his revelation though compelled to cease their overt activities. So Ndungumoi was banished to the island of Rotuma for ten years. In Rotuma, Ndungumoi married, living a quiet and unexceptionable life until, released and allowed to return to his native village, he died on board ship on his way back. Nevertheless, local rumour had it that Ndungumoi was once again demonstrating his extraordinary powers. Nobody at

home believed he had died. Later still, in 1892, one of Ndungumoi's original lieutenants claimed to have received letters
from him which had come from the sky. The sale of water began
again and the cult received fresh momentum.

The *Tuka* movement furnishes us with most of the classical
characteristics of a Melanesian cargo cult. And it also makes a
statement about the characteristics of a millenarian movement
anywhere. Dissatisfactions with a current redemptive process
and means of gaining prestige receive a political or quasi-
political expression; those in authority become nervous and call
it disaffection or even rebellion. A prophet emerges, a well-
travelled man who has had experience of other kinds of assumptions. He has a message which transcends the political solution.
It is a holistic solution. The millennium is expressed within a
particular cultural idiom; in this case access to European goods
and forms of power are brought into line with traditional
assumptions about power. If some elements of the wider community's assumptions are rejected, or impliedly rejected, other
elements are amalgamated or synthesized with the traditional.
European procedures such as drilling and marching, disciplined
activities from which power is derived, are adopted. The
prophet assumes a title which is a mixture of traditional and
European roles. In order to gain the promised benefits, whether
material, political or spiritual, money must be found and paid
over. Traditional economic concerns—or an economy on which
a traditional prestige system is based—are abandoned in the
hope or expectation of gaining a new one in which, presumably,
money and the goods it can buy will play the central part. In
acting out and exemplifying just this change-over from one
social order to another—by using money to give feasts—the
prophet reveals the meaning of cargo. Adherents are promised
plenty of everything within the terms of a new social order;
non-believers are sentenced to damnation. Myths are made;
traditional attitudes towards myths and dreams are used in
order to gain new ends; the political regime, however cunning
or apparently enlightened, cannot but add to the stature of the
prophet at the further expense of the bearers of the more
sophisticated social order; and at a later date the movement is
regenerated.

We may bear these characteristics in mind, perhaps reflecting on what might have happened if the administration had shown decisively where power lay. In the meanwhile let us go across miles of ocean to New Guinea.

THE KEKESI RITES, 1915[1]

The *Kekesi* rites, described by Chinnery,[2] whilst hardly a full-blooded millenarian movement, show up some facets of such a movement in embryo. One day a man named Bia, together with a friend, was returning to his native village after visiting kinsfolk and friends elsewhere. Stopping by the wayside for a rest, Bia had a vision of the spirit of a dead man—not in fact an unusual occurrence in New Guinea where men are expected to have encounters with the ghost of a dead father or elder brother.[3] In this instance the ghost or spirit offered to introduce Bia to *Kekesi*, a close friend of *Jesu Kerisu* (Jesus Christ). '*Kekesi* is going to make some new laws for the people', said the ghost of the dead man. 'If the people obey these laws then *Kekesi* will look after them. But if the people do not obey these laws then *Kekesi* will damage the crops and cut off all supplies of food.'[4] With that the ghost dissolved and Bia's experience came to an end.

A few nights later the ghost of the dead man again appeared to Bia, and this time introduced him to *Kekesi*. Bia was told to take careful note of what *Kekesi* had to say. *Kekesi* then went into a trance and started to recite his laws. But Bia could not understand what *Kekesi* was saying, and the ghost of the dead man had to interpret:

> You, Bia, are to tell the people that I am their chief, and they must obey me in all things. My wishes will be conveyed to them, my people, through you, Bia . . .

In brief, the people were to cultivate their gardens properly, and see that there was no waste. Disobedience would cause

[1] In Manua village on the Gira River in Papua.
[2] *Chinnery and Haddon*, pp. 452–4.
[3] Cf. above, p. 26—the old woman of the Cook Islands. See also *Lawrence* and *Meggitt*.
[4] Manua is a seaside village enjoying trading relations with Hanuabada, near Port Moresby.

interruptions in the food supply. Observing the traditional moral code, the people were to turn to the administrative authorities and obey them. Songs of praise were to be sung, to *Kekesi* frequently, and it was for Bia to prescribe how the songs should be sung and danced. When going to and from their work in the gardens, people should march in files, like police-boys. They should march smartly, neither strolling nor straggling. When at work certain commands (A-kush! A-shah!) should be given from time to time; failure to do so would endanger the ripening food crops. Travelling from place to place in a steamer, *Kekesi* would visit his people now and then to see that all was well.

The prophet Bia was a man well known to be subject to trances, fits and paroxysms whilst in a sitting position—a position similar to that which was reported as having been assumed by *Kekesi* when he was reciting the laws. Upon learning of this, and after seeing Bia do the same, others in the locality also became subject to paroxysms in a sitting position. The administration for its part, not over-apprehensive but clear that the paroxysms and rites were prejudicial to good order and discipline as understood by them, forbade both paroxysms and rites.

There is little need at the moment to proceed further with the description of the *Kekesi* activities. But some features deserve inspection. The rules or laws which were to guide members of the community in their relations with each other were, though disguised in a particular cultural idiom, for the people themselves and for Bia especially, plainly divinely inspired. They proceeded from a traditional type of non-human source, *Kekesi*, through the ghost of a dead man, and eventually through the prophet who articulated them to the community involved. Dealing with a traditional concern, the food supply, the laws were also clearly derived from those features of European culture and tradition, particularly administrative routines, which would have impinged most directly on the natives themselves: military precision, shouting orders, immediate obedience to orders, dislike of waste, authority—like the Administrator or Governor—moving about from place to place in a steamer. The songs sung by Bia seem to have been an amalgam of traditional melodies and Christian hymns.[1] If we rephrase these 'laws' in

[1] *Chinnery and Haddon.*

the idiom of European legislators they become a series of commandments which so rechannel traditional assumptions and ways as to embrace the most notable features of the new environment: an authoritarian political structure. Traditionally a gerontocratic democracy, the community can be seen as attempting to adopt a kind of organization and prestige system more consistent with the administrative organization and prestige system of their experience. This could, perhaps, have been done in some other way. But in fact, by means of a divine inspiration, a prophet adopted certain features of the European social order and articulated them to his fellows in the form of new rules relevant to a new and changing environment. He was rechannelling tradition, providing the opportunity for a new status within the wider community.

In the *Tuka* movement participants were exhorted to destroy their crops. An act of faith perhaps, but also the destruction of the basis of a subsistence economy in which money had no part, in which prestige was measured by qualities of industry and judgement in producing foodstuffs for a feast. And Ndungumoi symbolized the new order by himself using money as the basis for his prestige. In the *Kekesi* rites the crops were not destroyed. If the threatened failure of the food supply was a sanction encouraging or enforcing the members of the community to participate in the rites, playing the same role in principle as Ndungumoi's announcement that non-believers would be doomed to hell fire, the general tenor of the *Kekesi* rites still suggests a gradual development into a new condition of being rather than a sudden transformation. But in the *Baigona* cult, the *Taro* cult, and the *Vailala Madness*,[1] millenarian activities which followed hard on the heels of the *Kekesi* rites in the same area, this feature was reversed: the crops had to be destroyed if the new condition of being was to be realized. Drastic, perhaps, but in a sense realistic: a symbolic crossing of a Rubicon into a moneyed condition in which, like the Europeans, status would be wider and more generally significant.

What choice did the administration have? What might it have done about the *Kekesi* rites which would have made the later *Baigona* cult, *Taro* cult and *Vailala Madness* 'unnecessary'? The only answer seems to be that an administration,

[1] *Chinnery and Haddon*; *Williams, F. E.* (1), (2) and (3).

necessarily authoritative and responsible for keeping good order and peace, the apparent arbiter of the fates of whole communities, cannot but be involved in the total ambience of such activities. While the officers of an administration, looking down at their charges, may act 'correctly' or 'rightly' within their own terms of reference, in whatever manner they choose to exercise the powers at their disposal it is difficult to see how they might be 'correct' or 'right' in terms of the total situation. From being a body of exterior manipulators, at a distance from those whom they administrate, officials are forced by the movement to become a part of the developing situation. Just such a similarly active engagement with the administration would be necessary for a people who wanted to change their way of life otherwise than by a millenarian movement. While a powerful and ruthless regime would see to it that a proper distance was maintained, millenarian activities force a tolerant regime out of its hypocrisy, compel it to take notice. Either the administration is forced to join in the game—albeit in an oppositional role—or it must abdicate. In such circumstances the We/They opposition inherent in a colonial situation must resolve itself into Us: a single and synthesized total community.

MANAM ISLAND, 1952[1]

Though the *Kekesi* rites hardly amounted to a fully developed millenarian movement, there was a prophet, a revelation, and the attempt—within the positing of new assumptions—to come to terms with a new and changing environment. If we cannot but think of the *Kekesi* activities as a precursor to the much more coherent *Baigona* cult, *Taro* cult and *Vailala Madness*, movements that happen to have occurred later in time in the same region, we cannot know for certain whether the *Kekesi* rites were a necessary preliminary to these other movements. Each was self-justifying. There is no necessary causal connection between them. They seem simply to have happened, 'just-so'.

We turn now to consider how new assumptions begin to be generated in a community; and how, lacking a prophet in any obvious form, millenarian activities may still take place. The example is a personal anecdote.

[1] *Burridge* (2); idem (3), pp. 1–7.

One evening in 1952 as I was strolling homewards through the bush-lands of Manam Island, an islander emerged from the shrubs bordering the path and followed a few paces behind. 'Hum . . . Ha! Hum . . . Yes!' he murmured, as though imitating a punctilious civil servant. 'Hum . . . Okeydoke!' Stopping for a smoke, I offered the man some tobacco. 'Thank you, brother,' he said.

Then, after remarking on the weather, the islander said *'Mi save!* I understand!'

'What is it that you understand?'

In explanation the islander drew a diagram in the sand (p. 58). The dot in the middle, he said, was where *'Bigpela bolong ol gat up'*—where God or the Creator first manifested himself. About Him was snow in the upper layers, night, and day (represented by concentric circles). There was water. 'He' said the word and the lands came up. Drawing in the four cardinal points, the islander labelled them. Rabaul, Moresby, Manam, Aitape, Manus, Tokyo, North America, South America, England and Germany were identified and located, all in the Green sea around the cardinals. Then a triangle was scratched in the sand, offset from the cardinal labelled West. From England the White and Blue seas had to be crossed in order to get there.

'What is the name of this place?' I asked, pointing to the triangle.

'You know . . .' the islander replied craftily.

'But I do not know!'

'Oh yes, you do!' the islander insisted.

So and in such a way the islander continued to insist that I knew all about the place and its meaning, and since I knew, there was no need for him to tell me. Nevertheless, after continued fencing the islander admitted that no one in the world had seen this place or knew its name. Eventually described as 'far away and beyond the seas where everything could be learned and the good things of this world obtained' the triangle clearly represented some kind of *ultimum bonum*; and it is not impossible, from exterior evidence, that it might well have been known as Sewende, the Pidgin term for Seventh Day Adventists.[1]

[1] *Burridge* (2); *Burridge* (3), pp. 229–42, carries a full analysis of this incident.

The sand drawing may be thought of as a 'cargogram' or 'millenniagram': a graphical representation of the ambience of a Melanesian millenarian movement. Somewhere or somehow there is a state of plenty, a condition of being in which everything would be wholly understood, in which everything would be available to all. In more realistic political and economic

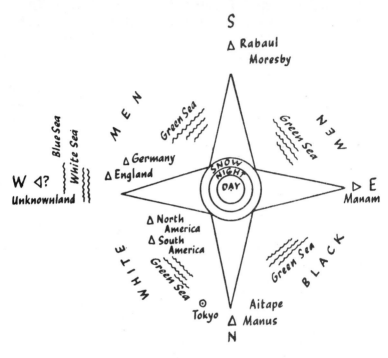

The Sand Drawing

terms, somewhere or somehow there is or could be equality of opportunity to comprehend power, equality of access to the world's goods, particularly European manufactured goods or cargo. But of course there are obstacles, represented here in the divides between the various seas, and in the explicit distinction between the worlds and abilities of black men and white. In Manam at that time Europeans tended to be seen in terms of their most evident and active symbol: the administration. In practice, the difficulties or obstacles to gaining access to the heart's desire tended to be concentrated not so much in Europeans in general as in the administration in particular.

One Manam islander, at about the same time as the incident described above occurred, hazarded the following:

> The Germans told us to do things—plant coconuts for instance—so that we could get some money. In those days money could buy something. Now it is not so—everything is too expensive. When the English came we were just rubbish—poor. We had to stay like that. We have only the things we have always had. If the Germans had stayed I think we would have had everything.

Another man said:

> We do not understand. We are just in the middle. First the Germans came—and the Australians pushed them out. Then the Japanese pushed the Australians out. Later, the Australians and Americans got rid of the Japanese. It is beyond us. When an administrative officer tells us to carry his gear and goods we have to do it. When a German or Japanese told us to carry his goods we had to do it. If we did not they might kill us. . . .

There was in Manam Island at the time a man of great ability named Irakau. But he was not, nor had he been, a prophet. He had had no message, no revelation. Being able, and realizing the value of money in an economy and social order made possible by a particular attitude towards money, he had planted coconuts, made his own copra, and then started to sell his merchandize within the European markets. Seeing him prosper, others had joined him, becoming his partners in the enterprise. As he gathered dependants and followers in his prosperity—a quite traditional occurrence—he also attracted others, more mystically inclined, who tried to push him into the role of prophet. But this role Irakau steadfastly refused to accept. He was a businessman, wielding decisive political influence in his community, with unmatched prestige through most of the island. Yet there were some villages where Irakau's success had engendered feelings of envy and bitterness. And in these places there were those who would have preferred him to become a prophet. For while as a successful businessman, doing what others might have done, he made the less able look small, as a prophet he would have transcended local and sectional political rivalries and brought a general new order and prosperity in his train. Those who were trying to push Irakau into the role of a prophet had more than a mystical emotionalism behind them. And, because Manam islanders were in fact waiting for just such a prophet,[1] had Irakau yielded to the importunings of some of his associates there is little doubt that he would have taken the whole island with him. But Irakau remained adamant, content with what he was, and in what he was doing.

Having seen the kind of activity that may take place where no prophet as such emerges, let us return again to consider the role of the administration. In stopping the *Kekesi* rites administrative officers may well have congratulated themselves on timely, moderate and efficient action. They could not have foreseen the much more violent *Vailala Madness* and *Taro* cult that were to come. With the benefit of hindsight, what advice might have been given to the administration in relation to the *Tuka* activities? Making the prophet into either a 'hero' or a 'martyr' were surely their only alternatives. In Manam Island, at about the same time as the incidents described above, an administrative officer, being zealous in his work and thinking to forestall possible troubles, and knowing that flowers in vases were almost sure indications in the area of imminent cargo activity, set himself the task of looking for just these signs. Realizing, however, that the officer was looking for flowers in vases, Manam islanders not only determined to hide them from him, but became more convinced than they had been that there must be some exceptional magical potency in arranging flowers in vases. This might well be the very secret of European dominion and superior capacities for which they were looking. Given that an administration tends to subsume all the obstacles to comprehension, learning and plenty, what more likely than that its officers should prevent the islanders from gaining access to comprehension, learning and plenty? Elsewhere in New Guinea, again at about the same time, the administration, thinking to 'capture' an incipient movement and so bend the energies released to what it considered more 'constructive' tasks, gave the prophet in question its full support. But it was not long before the support had to be withdrawn, the prophet imprisoned, and the activities suppressed.[2] To have allowed things to continue would have been prejudicial to peace and good order.

[1] *Burridge* (3), pp. 1–4.
[2] I have in mind Yali's activities. Below, pp. 68–9.

Because, as has been suggested, an administration becomes
an integral part of the total ambience of a set of millenarian
activities,[1] the results of its operations tend to be little surer
than those of the activities themselves. Yet since all millenarian
activities must be in some part challenging, rebellious or revolutionary, an administration must seek either to contain or
insulate them, or it must suppress them. The result is that
whether or not the activities in question are initially directed
against the administration, they always end up by appearing
to be so. And it is this feature which so often obscures the fact
that millenarian activities tend to be 'inner' rather than 'outer'
directed, are a protest or rebellion against a community's own
condition first, and only later identify, and set themselves
against, those who appear to be preventing the shift into a new
way of life. There is no evidence of opposition to Europeans or
their principles of authority in the *Kekesi* rites and *Siovili*
activities—rather the reverse. Though the *Pai-marire* movement expressed in a classical way opposition both to Europeans
and their principles of authority, these were secondary to the
redemption of a people who had become 'forgetful, desolate and
in doubt'. In opposing Europeans, participants in the *Tuka*
movement yet sought to take over from the Europeans their
principles of authority. In the eyes of his followers Ndungumoi
had gained the status of a European and was able to outwit
Europeans on their own ground. But the common and decisive
element in these activities is surely brought out in the Cook
Islands cult: the right to assert, and have duly recognized,
qualities of manhood and moral being. No less than the old lady
and her adherents, the man who refused to be 'baptized in
Satan' showed his quality and integrity and, perversely perhaps, vindicated the cult.

[1] A brief footnote to the millenarian ambience and its persuasiveness.
I once showed a photograph to a Melanesian in the near neighbourhood
of Manam island. The photograph depicted a typical New Guinea scene:
a boy standing in front of his hut, holding a piglet under his arm. 'What
do you think of this?' I asked. The man studied the photograph for a
moment and then returned it, saying firmly: 'This is a picture of Christ
riding into Jerusalem on a donkey!'

6

Historical Interconnections

One of the classic dilemmas of an historian is the fixing of a starting point. We must allow that there have been millenarian activities which have generated themselves *de novo*. But only rarely can we be sure that there are no connections whatever with similar kinds of movement either through a direct historical link, or through a common tradition: two kinds of linkage between which it is useful to maintain a formal distinction. If an aircraft passing over the New Guinea Highlands can trigger off a series of activities of a millenarian kind, then even though the aircraft itself can be considered a product of the Christian tradition the connection is so tenuous that we must allow of social processes that may be complementary to, but independent of, traditional or historical connections. We can trace the origins of the *Pai-marire* in the King movement, and we can discover the *Pai-marire* in the *Ringatau* religious sect. The founder of the *Ringatau* was a member of the *Pai-marire*, and participants in the *Pai-marire* were also involved in the King movement. At the same time, apart from a common if developing exposure to Christian or European ways, it is useful to bear in mind that the historical connections do not of themselves account for either the *Pai-marire* or the *Ringatau*. We must allow that something akin to what happened in the New Guinea Highlands when an aircraft was sighted also happened in the region of the Waikato. After all, there were other Maori in other parts of New Zealand who had suffered much the same exposure to European and Christian ways as had those in the Waikato, but among whom there were no millenarian movements.

We may surmise, but we do not know, that there were historical connections between the *Kekesi* rites, the *Taro* cult, the *Baigona* cult, and the *Vailala Madness*. Since the participants in these several movements were all members of a common culture area where there was a great deal of intercommunication and news gathering, we can assume that as each set of activities took place others in the area came to know what had occurred and followed the example of their neighbours. Yet because on the face of it each successive congregation of participants was following an example that did not, again on the face of it, yield very much, we are left with more questions to answer. If we forego a refuge in the acknowledged historical fact that most chiliasms outlive their enthusiastic period and, in spite of disappointed expectations, settle down into a sectarian existence, we must ask in what senses expectations are *not* disappointed in those cases where, in a particular area, movements occur and recur. Also, in pointing to a common exposure to Christian missionaries and European ways we must ask why others, with a like exposure, did not participate in millenarian activities. Remembering the aircraft flying over the New Guinea Highlands, it begins to look as though social processes which are independent of historical connections or a common tradition must exist. Because in many instances we know what happened before and after a millenarian movement took place, we feel bound to seek for an overall pattern. But the possibility that the pattern is merely contingent must continually be borne in mind.

Nevertheless, all millenarian movements must have had some kind of beginning, and the incidents on Manam Island, described above, give us an idea of how a movement may start. Puzzled and anxious or uncertain about the ways things are, individuals begin to rationalize, posit alternatives, seek the assumptions which will bring order to the present and give assurance about the future. We may now enlarge on this process of beginning and development by referring to two series of activities that took place in the Madang District of New Guinea. Themselves interconnected in a direct historical sense, each nevertheless takes departure from a common collection of myths. And when we speak of 'myths' in the Melanesian context, bizarre and esoteric though they may seem we are speaking of formulations with the same kind of doctrinal force in relation to basic assumptions as, for example, the Book of Revelations,[1] or St. Paul's letters to the Corinthians.[1]

[1] Cf. *Cohn*, pp. 1–33; *Rogers*, p. 5.   [2] Cf. *Knox*, Ch. 2.

TANGU

The first case concerns an inland community known as Tangu,[1] whose initial direct contacts with Europeans occurred shortly before the first world war. No doubt they had known about Europeans for some years; no doubt individuals had gone down to the coast to see, and work for, Europeans. Quite early in their European experience, Tangu explained the presence and capacities of Europeans, and the latter's relations with themselves, in the form of a myth. Once upon a time, the story goes, there were two brothers. One was the ancestor of white men, the other the ancestor of black men. But because of an act by a mythical ancestor, the killing of a snake or eel, one of the brothers was well endowed with brains, ability and inventiveness, whilst the other was dull and could only copy. The clever brother was the ancestor of white men, and seems to have represented white men as a class; the duller brother was the ancestor of black men, representing black men as a class.

Two points may be noted. First, the myth is so similar to other myths current along the northern coast of New Guinea, and reported as early as 1867—particularly the myth, known as the Mansren myth, originating from Biak in West Irian[2]—that, notwithstanding the fact that myths about elder and younger brothers are common all over Melanesia, it is at least possible that parts of the myth were imported into Tangu. Second, in Tangu itself an explanatory gloss in the shape of alternative interpretations became attached to the myth. Some saw the predicament of the dull brother as permanent. Others held that since the two men were in fact brothers, and brothers normally shared their assets, white men would come round to sharing their goods, privileges and capacities with black men. Thirdly, there were those who felt that if the clever brother did not share his assets, then he might be forced to do so or be made to withdraw from New Guinea. It is within terms of this 'doctrinal' background that we should perhaps understand the historical fact that missionary activity among the Tangu people was at first resented, and then welcomed. The initial opposition to coming under the supervision of strangers melted when it was felt that the myth might be being realized in terms of the

[1] *Burridge* (3).   [2] *Bruijn.*

second alternative: assets were going to be shared; clever brother had come to Tangu to teach them how they might gain access to the goods, privileges and capacities of white men. Yet, as the years passed and nothing very dramatic happened, there were some who felt that the whole business of sharing a common pool of assets was going suspiciously slowly. These men did not want to wait, and for them the third alternative gloss began to make headway. They were ready for the emergence of a prophet. And in 1937 Mambu appeared.[1] The gist of Mambu's message was that either white men should be forced to share their assets now, or that they should be made to withdraw from New Guinea. He also prescribed certain rites and procedures which, he assured his followers, would bring about either of these desiderata.

The missionaries in Tangu reacted immediately to Mambu's activities there, and he was forced to go elsewhere, to the coast. Here he started a movement whose features exemplify a typical cargo movement. Mambu assumed the title of 'Black King'. He asserted that the deities responsible for making manufactured goods had already despatched them to black men, but that white men had intercepted the packages and changed the labels —redirecting the cargo to themselves. Collecting contributions in cash, Mambu told his followers that if they would do as he advised a ship laden with manufactured goods for all would arrive in due course. Those who ignored his advice would be swallowed in a holocaust. Mambu and his adherents erected a sacred building upon which they placed a red flag and cruciform; and in or by it recruits to the movement were 'baptized' by having their genitals sprinkled with water, breechclouts and skirts having been stripped off beforehand and buried. Promiscuous sexual intercourse is said to have taken place. After 'baptism' the faithful donned European clothing, a procedure, Mambu said, that the ancestors had very much at heart. But despite this traditional warrant for the adoption of European ways, Mambu also exhorted his followers not to co-operate with Christian missionaries and not to comply with administrative orders and instructions. He himself spent much of his time

---

[1] *Höltker*; *Worsley*, pp. 104–8; *Burridge* (3). Mambu was not a Tangu man. He was a stranger from the coast and seems to have been acceptable to Tangu because he was a stranger. (*Burridge* (3), pp. 254–66).

praying, as the missionaries had taught him. But in doing so in
the village cemetery, addressing himself to the ancestors, he
gave a new way a traditional context.

As Mambu's movement gathered momentum the administration found themselves forced to take action. Mambu was gaoled
and the movement was broken up. On the surface, affairs
returned to their normal routine. But of course, as we might
have come to expect, this was by no means the end of the matter.
Mambu had but stirred a pre-existing ferment. Like Te Ua in
New Zealand, Mambu had been a promising mission convert to
Christianity and, despite occasional odd behaviour, had
impressed his teachers with his apparent piety. Like Te Ua
again, and like Ndungumoi in Fiji, Mambu was credited with
miraculous powers. And after he himself had faded from the
scene his supposed adventures and capacities—which may or
may not have been woven out of actual occurrences seen somewhere—were spun into a myth or legend which was itself to
play an important part in the millenarian activities in which
Tangu eventually engaged.[1]

The Japanese invaded New Guinea and administration became sporadic. Then, with the victory in the field of the Ameri-
cans and Australians, there was a brief prosperity as Tangu
shared in the spoils of war. Afterwards came the return to
normal routine under the supervision of missionaries and a fresh
Australian administration. War damage compensation put
plenty of money into native hands, but it was soon spent on
manufactured goods at inflated prices. Then a familiar question
arose. How to continue earning money without anything to sell?
How to gain a regular access to manufactured goods without
money to buy them? In the 1950s, under the impetus provided
by a renowned and able prophet named Yali—whom we shall
encounter again presently—but under the direct influence
of two minor prophets to whom a series of rites were revealed in dreams, Tangu engaged in two sets of overt cargo
activities.

There is no need to deal with these activities in detail here.
It is sufficient to point to four separate prophets, three occurrences of millenarian activity, one people, and a single developing theme. Like any other prophet, Mambu articulated certain

[1] *Burridge* (1); (3), pp. 182–96.

aspirations. And there is little doubt that his relevance at the time to the peoples concerned drew sustenance from the myth about the two brothers. Where particular individuals might have been doubtful about which gloss or interpretation to put on the myth, Mambu gave them certainty. A prosperous future and a new and worthwhile kind of redemption were made to look secure. Imprisoned at the height of his reputation, and thus preserved from the temptations and falterings that are almost inevitably a part of a prophet's later experience, Mambu became a hero. And in the myth or legend about him that eventually developed, three points are worth remark.[1] First, he was credited with learning and understanding. Second, he was reputed to have been able to get money whenever he wanted to do so by mystical means. Third, in his legendary adventures which took him to Australia by ship, he outwitted hostile Europeans, in particular the captain of the ship; and with the help of friendly Europeans, a planter and his sister, he was enabled to gain access to cargo. The first and second points we might by now have come to expect. But the third point bears some further inspection.

In the myth about the brothers, Europeans appear as undifferentiated, as Europeans simply, as white-skinned folk with qualities of inventiveness and capacities of understanding and initiative, as a class of people roughly defined by their unlimited access to cargo or manufactured goods. With the myth about Mambu they are differentiated into two categories: inimical Europeans and friendly Europeans. While Mambu the man may be said to have interpreted the myth about the two brothers in terms of the third alternative—that because Europeans would not share their assets they should be forced to withdraw from New Guinea—the Mambu of myth acted in terms of a synthesis between the second and third alternatives. That is, though some Europeans will continue hostile, others will come round to sharing their assets with black brother. And these friendly Europeans, it is implied, will help their black brothers by persuading other white folk to share their goods. Not only may we see here the kind of synthesis we have come to expect, but within this synthesis a process of increasing differentiation. We begin to appreciate the significance of the friendly

[1] *Burridge* (3), pp. 188–96.

Europeans, or what we may call the 'moral European'.[1] He is not only friendly or moral, but a point of entry into that highly differentiated community characterized by money. The purely racial elements in the situation begin to dissolve. The political and economic controllers—who have money and goods, to whom money always returns, and who seem to seek to prevent a regular access to money—are distinguished from the sharers, moral Europeans, who will provide this access. In the myth about Mambu those who helped him did so by giving him cargo, money, and a letter which could protect him from possible misfortunes. It becomes clear that moral Europeans are figured as doing what they can to help their black brothers realize that new condition of being which is predicated by writing, a regular access to money, and the goods that only money can buy.

The theme of the moral European is an important one. It shows that within the local millenarian ambience Europeans in general were to be defined less by the colour of their skins and more by their access to money and manufactured goods. The moral European bridges the gap between two radically opposed conditions of being: the inimical European with an access to money and goods which he will not share, and the black man who has neither goods nor the money to buy them. With the capacities of a white man, but adopting the relatively un-differentiated and idealized moral attitudes of the black man, the moral European is the obverse of the prophet who symbolizes the new man: the black man who has European capacities, who is worthy of the new kind of redemptive process which the European conditions of life entail.

It is within this context that we can best understand the impact of the prophet Yali, the man under whose influence Tangu engaged in their later cargo activities. Yali had been a policeman, then a soldier, and was decorated for his gallantry during the war. Recognizing his ability, the administration recruited Yali into the service in a special role, believing that this would be a useful experiment and example in persuading New Guineans to shoulder administrative responsibilities. Later, though the administration broke with him for a variety of reasons, Yali earned the grudging respect of those Europeans

[1] *Burridge* (3), pp. 240–70.

who regarded him with undisguised hostility. Thus, not simply
influential among his own kind, Yali had earned and gained
prestige within the European ambience. In many respects he
had become like a European, he had broken into their prestige
system. To Tangu, therefore, Yali had begun to realize the
promise of Mambu. But in addition to his acknowledged prestige among Europeans, Yali's relevance as a prophet can only
be fully appreciated within the millenarian context, particularly in the light of the myth about the two brothers, the activities of Mambu the man, and the myth about Mambu's supposed
activities. Given this socio-historical perspective, the rites and
activities advocated by the two minor prophets (who actually
triggered the Tangu activities of the early fifties), gain further
meaning. For these rites symbolized the making of a new man,
a black man with European abilities and capacities of understanding, a black man enjoying European conditions of being.[1]
Yali conformed to this image. Having become a man of standing in the total environment, having to a certain extent realized
the greater integrity, he exemplified a new redemption.

SOUTHERN MADANG DISTRICT

The Southern Madang district of New Guinea is well known as
an area in which cargo or millenarian movements are likely to
occur. They have been taking place in the region for over
seventy years. Yet so long as investigators continued to follow
the administration—which could hardly have done otherwise—
in regarding each occurrence pragmatically and on its own as a
unique occasion, then for so long were the possible interconnections missed. Now, however, as a result of the investiga-
tions of Dr. P. Lawrence,[2] we know that all the movements in
this area of New Guinea must have been interconnected. News,
rumours, myths and legends travelled fast over a wide area, and
these provided the basis for an intellectual and emotional ferment which expressed itself in a variety of activities up and
down the district. Lawrence was able to identify five developmental stages. Among the many prophets who came forward
from time to time there were rivalries and disagreements—

[1] *Burridge* (3), pp. 1–13, 202–28.
[2] *Lawrence* (2).

features with which historians of our own enthusiastic or millenarian periods are quite familiar.[1]

The first stage identified by Lawrence, lasting from about
1871 to 1900, was one in which the natives of the area attempted
to understand Europeans and their own experience of Europeans directly in terms of their own traditions. Thus the first
Europeans of their acquaintance were identified as deities or
culture heroes, the bearers of untold wealth and superhuman
knowledge. The cycles of creation and recreation as related in
their myths had the appearance of being realized in their own
generation. The time when man would at last be at one with
himself and his gods seemed to be at hand. In a little while,
however, as land began to be sequestrated and as the villagers
began to be treated with a certain brusqueness, it became clear
that the final redemption had not arrived yet. A distinction was
made between those first comers who, like the mythical heroes,
had brought gifts, and those who followed and insisted upon
taking as well as, or in preference to, giving. A traditional myth
about two culture heroes, often brothers, who had sailed down
the Madang coast distributing varieties of traditional goods,
provided an appropriate basis of received truths within which
to understand the activities of Europeans. Still a little daunted
by white men, and not too familiar with them, the natives were
trying to fit their visitors into a traditional framework of
assumptions and expectations.

The next stage, from about 1900 to 1914, saw a development
of myths, a developing doctrine about Europeans. Though they
still tried to understand the much wider culture within the
terms of a much smaller and narrower set of ideas, varieties of
interpretation had begun to centre on two versions of a myth.
This, going along similar lines to the myth about the two
brothers which we have already noted, purported to account for
the power of Europeans. But, having discovered that Europeans
could be killed by traditional native weapons, and that they
themselves could use European guns to kill Europeans, it
became clear that Europeans were not deities or even like
deities. They were mere human beings who could be made to
suffer the same kinds of fate as other human beings. On the
other hand, it was equally evident that Europeans were human

[1] Cf. *Cohn*; *Knox*; *Fulop-Miller*; *Rogers*.

beings with extraordinary capacities. They alone controlled the source of European goods.

It was within this context that the third stage developed. Taking it for granted—in accordance with traditional assumptions—that European goods were made by deities, it was clear that these deities were not the traditional culture heroes, but the European deities, God and Jesus Christ. More accurately, since the natives were well aware that they themselves and not their deities actually made their own traditional artifacts, the sources of that power which enabled Europeans to have an exclusive access to their goods were God and Jesus Christ.[1] Further, the general friendliness of Christian missionaries seemed to be evidence that, whatever other kinds of European might feel or do, the missionaries at least would honour the ties of brotherhood. They would reveal to New Guineans the secret rituals which would ensure that God and Jesus Christ would enable the people of New Guinea to have access to supplies of cargo. God, it was thought, had said to the missionaries:

> Your brothers in New Guinea are lost in the darkness. They have no cargo because of Ham's folly. But now I am sorry for them and want to help them. You missionaries, therefore, must go to New Guinea and undo Ham's mistake. You must win over his descendants to my ways again. When they follow me again, I shall send them cargo in the same way as I send it to you white men now.[2]

With this as the firstfruits of their teaching, European missionaries began to establish themselves with greater assurance. More mission stations were built, conversions increased, schools began to fill with the young. The gardener or fisherman who had only known the ideas and social relationships contained within his own village community began to enter the intellectual, if not the political, economic and technological ambience of European civilization. Consequently, with the fourth stage of development many Christian features are to be found. Bits and pieces of the new learning became welded to traditional ways of thought and conducting relationships. New Guineans were beginning to synthesize. It was in this stage, at the point when they were beginning to syncretize, that most of the millenarian activities in the area took place.

[1] My paraphrasing of Lawrence's material.   [2] *Lawrence* (2), p. 77.

Placing the third stage between 1914 and 1933, the fourth stage takes us through the years of the great European economic depression to the end of the Japanese war. The fifth stage was a phase of disillusionment. Following upon experiences with the Japanese and the euphoric optimisms of the immediate post-war period when, with war damage compensation in their hands and stocks of abandoned war supplies lying around, goods seemed to be arriving in profusion, there was not so much a reversal to traditional or pagan rites as a rejection of the kind of Christianity they had been receiving. While the intellectual content of Christian teaching and the European experience could scarcely be thrown overboard, much of the formal ritual—such as attendances at church and school—was discarded. Villagers began inventing their own forms of Christianity.[1] Yali arrived on the scene. Hitherto, local movements and sets of activities had been set in motion by local prophets who had found acceptance only among relatively small groups of people. Yali was able to transcend the many local exclusivisms typical of the New Guinea scene. Already widely travelled, he made a point of touring the countryside, going from village to village. Minor prophets, would-be prophets and local men of affairs waited on his visits, sought his advice, discussed the situation with him. Not all of these local leaders were wholly enchanted with Yali, but, as we have seen, it was through one of these visits of Yali's that Tangu themselves, among whom a millenarian ambience had been developing for many years, actually engaged in cargo activities at the direct instigation of two minor prophets.

Now though the political relationships between Yali and the many minor prophets he encountered have not, as yet, been ascertained with any clarity, there seems little doubt that as he matured Yali tried to become a political leader rather than a prophet.[2] With his relatively wider knowledge and experience of the outside world, and remembering his connection with the administration, it was perhaps to be expected that Yali's ambitions would be more closely associated with matter-of-fact political aspirations than with the transcendence expected of a prophet. Yet in the former respect Yali had little lasting im-

[1] Cf. *Burridge* (3), p. 7.
[2] Compare Irakau, above, pp. 59–60.

pact. His charisma, his hold on those who knew and followed him, seems to have derived from the millenarian ambience alone. Stripped of this aura, one feels, he would simply have been a capable man, quite unacceptable as an overall political leader until he had demonstrated in each community his ability to command labour and allegiance on the one hand, and to provide the goods which showed his command on the other. In fact, if Yali was not to retire into obscurity, as had so many of his predecessors, he had to respond to the popular behest that he should be something very much more than himself. So, wearing his mantle with some dignity, though Yali never seems actually to have promised a complete transcendence of the political difficulties, he allowed his followers to believe that he had such a promise in mind.[1]

POSSIBILITIES AND PROBABILITIES

New Guinea is a mountainous country, difficult to traverse. Yet in spite of the existence of hundreds of small communities with different languages, news travels fast and the core of a consensus of attitude builds firmly and quickly. European penetration, on the other hand, has been gradual, slow, and uneven both in time and in space. With the wisdom of hindsight we might expect the appearance of apparently separate sets of activities. But, as the examples above have shown, in New Guinea—as indeed in Europe, Asia, Africa and the Americas—there are wide areas of historical interconnectedness. The overt and visible activities which attract notice, and become named this or that cult or movement, are the outward manifestations of an overall developmental process. Chiliasms tend to outlive the apparent non-fulfilment of their prophesies because the failure to gain the millennium is in itself, given the ambience, a guarantee that the activities will occur again or continue in more muted form. Few prophets cannot be seen to have had precursors, and in some areas prophets follow one upon the other. In developing and exampling an image of the new man, prophets enable their followers to define what they are and might be. It is the new man that must be realized, not necessarily access to manufactured goods, invulnerability and so on. The several revelations

[1] *Lawrence* (2), pp. 116–222.

of successive prophets are attempts to realize the imperatives of the new man. Doubt and uncertainty are intolerable, must give way to commitment. Once a new redemptive process has been envisaged, realizing the new man in a new moral order becomes a compelling force. It must be attempted.

By and large the peoples of New Guinea have had much the same sorts of experience of Europeans. Without taking historical interconnections into account it would be difficult to explain why there have not been many more millenarian movements in New Guinea. Given one or two sources it is relatively simple to derive others from these, and the latter from the messianism inherent in Christianity. Yet even were we to take account of every millenarian movement that had ever occurred, finding a single source for them all, we would still be telling little more than a just-so story. History provides us with some basis for saying why there have not been many more movements. But it cannot tell us why movements did not occur, nor does it tell us why particular movements should have occurred when they did. If some clues are to be found in neuro-physiological conditions,[1] as sociologists we are debarred, even if competent, from taking them into account. On the other hand, the evidence does suggest a way out of the dilemma of historicism on the one hand, and biological or psychological reductionism on the other.[2] The historical perspective shows these movements to be in some way symptomatic of an overall developmental process. Given this knowledge we are forced to approach the problem in a roughly statistical way. We have to think of the possibilities and probabilities which seem to be inherent in the general pattern of developing social relations. Within this context a particular history is vital. It provides the evidence with which to fill in the content of the new man, the redemptive process, competing assumptions, prestige, and the retention of integrity. It enables us to develop and qualify the general framework. And this in itself helps us to see in what ways the different cultural idioms are expressing much the same things.

[1] Below, pp. 119–20.   [2] Below, pp. 119–22.

7
Aspects of Integrity

All cultures and communities have particular criteria whereby members may measure relative prestige among themselves. As we have seen very briefly, among Polynesians a variety of criteria meet in the meaning of *mana*, command over the labour and allegiance of others, and competence in war. Other kinds of ability certainly contribute to the accumulation of *mana*: knowledge of protocol and myths, sexual competence, physical strength, handsome features, well-moulded muscular proportions, oratory, and skills in dancing, sports, sailing, fishing, hunting, agricultural activities and the manufacture of artifacts, to name but a few. But all these qualities tend to be subsumed in the required qualities of the political leader and warrior. And the basis of both these competences was control over land and its resources. A landless fellow, a man without any control over its resources, was necessarily a man without kin, or one whom others would not recognize as kin: scarcely a man at all. When Te Ua claimed to hold the promise of a 'redemption for his people, who had become forgetful, desolate and in doubt'[1] his meaning in an objective sense must be related to the land question and to warfare. As accessible and useful lands began to shrink, and as traditional warfare began to become difficult or impossible within the context of a *Pax Britannica*, so the criteria of relative prestige became less and less clearly defined.

Not only that. For as the criteria of prestige become loose and ill-defined, so do the criteria of integrity become doubtful. The kinds of powers attached to a particular office or status become uncertain. There is no consensus as to the qualities required of those in positions of authority and responsibility. Further, traditional criteria of integrity tend to seem unimportant when compared with the apparently superior capacities of other

[1] Above, p. 17.

peoples—in this case the European settlers. Whether we choose to regard the *Pai-marire* movement as one that attempted to capture a new integrity; or as one that attempted to recapture a traditional integrity; or as one that attempted to define an integrity compounded of both traditional and Christian or European features; the question of integrity emerges as paramount. This itself is bound up with the redemptive process, the programme of particular kinds of ways in which individuals are required to meet their obligations.

In a millenarian context both redemption and integrity are part and parcel of an overall developmental process—a movement from the more simple to the more complex, an increasing differentiation of the powers, statuses, qualities, jobs and techniques required to sustain community life. But we still have to show how varying aspects of integrity and redemption are related to different kinds of developmental process. Some examples from North America and India will demonstrate my meaning.

THE PLAINS INDIANS

For something over two hundred years until their final defeat by the white man, the cultures of the Plains Indians of North America had been based on possession of the horse, fighting, and hunting wild buffalo. Before the Spanish brought their horses to North America, the indigenous peoples of the region had lived mainly on the edges of the plains, and comprised small hunting bands who followed the migrating herds of buffalo in the season on foot. They also practised some horticulture. But when they acquired horses they were able to take to the plains more or less permanently, relying for subsistence almost wholly on the buffalo. The population increased; the size of the effective political group increased. From being a motley collection of small hunting bands who could only have put up a token resistance to the white pioneers, they became the well-organized and formidable antagonists of an industrialized nation. They had neither artillery nor the means to manufacture guns and bullets. But they acquired guns and ammunition and fought for their plains and their buffalo until only a few remnants remained. Looking back, we can see that their fight against white men, who wanted the plains for farmland and range cattle, was doomed to failure. Yet they had fought according to the demands of their culture. And those who died bravely may be said to have earned a traditional redemption: they asked only that they should show themselves true to the prescriptions of their social order. But what of those who survived?

Of the many changes that possession of the horse initiated, the most crucial related to integrity and relative prestige. Horses became the new wealth. Gaining access to horses by taking them from enemies either by stealth or in open war became an important criterion of prestige. Getting horses by breeding them was tantamount to forgery. Warrior values became paramount. The dashing fighter who could get horses, count coups, gallop in amongst a herd of bewildered buffalo, and face extremes of physical pain in stoic silence, was well on the way to a position of high success. Add to these abilities qualities of wisdom, magnanimity, cunning, knowledge of the world and his people, and a certain ruthlessness, and the picture of the Plains Indian chief is complete in its outlines. At the other extreme, a male who could not show some competence in these matters was regarded as hardly a man at all. His alternatives were either to become a shaman, when again he would have to show himself able to face without flinching extremes of physical pain and deprivation; or become like a woman—dress in woman's clothes, do women's work, become a disposable part of a real man's household. Highly specialized, the prestige system was based on an intimate relationship between war, buffalo and horses. Death in war, fighting and dying bravely without asking for, or giving, quarter was thought a highly satisfactory redemption. To die peacefully having survived innumerable combats with a fully feathered war-bonnet and coups past counting; to have hunted successfully, fed dependants, and disposed of plenty of horses; to have fingers whose joints had been severed in attempts to gain visions of, and rapport with, a protector spirit; to bare a torso scarred with the hooks and skewers of voluntary torture—all these were tokens of a perhaps higher redemption.

What then was left for those remnants who lived through to the end of the Indian wars in reservations without horses, without buffalo, without war, dependent on the goodwill of an official agent, a trader with his store, and perhaps a missionary?

Even as we look back with the advantage of hindsight it is not easy to suggest a realistic compromise for this brave but defeated people. To them defeat was a disgrace. But they had to live on in defeat and they were denied the opportunity of living and dying in the only fit ways they knew. In their own eyes rather less than men, despite assurances to the contrary their conquerors treated them with undisguised contumely. How and in what way could they overcome the irony of a glorious efflorescence based on the horse, a European import, and their ultimate defeat by Europeans? How and in what way could they find a new integrity, a new redemption?

In a sense there was no solution. Plains Indian culture was dead, could not develop into anything else. If in later years descendants of these folk could point to the fact that all the world plays at Cowboys and Indians, this simply reiterates the problem for the immediate survivors. Bereft of a traditional integrity, the scattered remnants of a once proud people could do little else but look back on their glories and, with the aid of some new symbols, screw hope and wishful thinking to the point where buffalo and horses might seem to be on the point of returning. For the Sioux, who were to suffer so dreadfully at the battle of Wounded Knee, one version of the many revelations contributed by numerous prophets to that complex of activities generally subsumed under the name 'Ghost Dance Religion'[1] posited a general catastrophe as heralding the millennium. After a series of earthquakes, landslides, storms, whirlwinds and floods in which all the whites would be destroyed, the Indians would survive to see boundless prairies covered with wild grass and filled with great herds of buffalo and other game. Other prophets held that after the great catastrophe all race distinctions were to be obliterated, and that in the millennium that followed both whites and Indians would live amicably together. 'You must not fight. Do not harm anyone. Do right always,'[2] said the prophet Wovoka.

A longer text from Wovoka's teaching reads as follows:

I found my children were bad, so I went back to heaven and left them. I told them that in so many hundred years I would come back to see my children. At the end of this time I was sent back to

---

[1] *Mooney.*   [2] *Mooney*, p. 19.

try to teach them. My father told me the earth was getting old and worn out and the people getting bad, and that I was to *renew everything as it used to be and make it better.*

He also told us that all our dead were to be resurrected; that they were all to come back to earth, and that, as the earth was too small for them and us, he would do away with heaven and make the earth itself large enough to contain us all; that we must tell all the people we met about these things. He spoke to us about *fighting,* and said *that was bad and we must keep from it;* that the earth was to be all good hereafter, and *we must all be friends with one another.* He said that in the fall of the year the youth of all good people would be renewed, so that nobody would be more than forty years old, and that if they behaved themselves well after this *the youth of everyone would be renewed* in the spring. He said if we were all good he would send people among us who could heal all our wounds and sickness by mere touch and that we would *live forever.* He told us *not to quarrel or fight or strike each other, or shoot one another;* that the whites and Indians were to be *all one people.* He said if any man *disobeyed* what he ordered his tribe would be *wiped from the face of the earth;* that we must believe everything he said, and we must not doubt him or say he lied; that if we did, he would know it; that *he would know our thoughts and actions in no matter what part of the world we might be.*[1]

Here plainly is the attempt to excise the purely existential and apparently purposeless nature of the present by searching into the past in order to posit a viable future.

The Ghost Dance Religion spread from community to community in the plains area in much the same way as cargo cult activities have in more recent years spread from village to village in New Guinea. And in spite of Mooney's insistence on what was the 'true' or 'real' doctrine of the Ghost Dance Religion, it is probably wiser to accept that here (as in New Guinea and elsewhere) there were different versions; differently projected assumptions and aspirations turning on the central theme of a glorious past and miserably uncertain future. On the other hand the rites of the Ghost Dance itself, which included singing, chanting, falling into trance, stripping naked, and the wearing of special shirts which would render the wearers invulnerable to the bullets of the white man, seem to have varied only slightly. Also, the overt purposes of the rites seem to have been

[1] *Mooney,* pp. 26–7 (my italics).

much the same: attaining union with the glorious dead, enjoying now in trance what in the past had been fully realized.
Moreover, if we look closely at the Ghost Dance we can discern
certain themes—(such as trance, self-torture, the excision of
discordant ideas, the renewal and re-emphasis of community
values, the reconciliation of disputants)—which it had in
common with the great Sun Dance: that vital political occasion
when nomadic bands of Indians gathered together to dance,
feast, resolve their disputes, compete in games and ritual exercises of self-torture, and, despite or because of their sectional
exclusivisms, renew their common allegiance to an overall
political order.[1] Thus the Ghost Dance was heir to the Sun
Dance; the traditional gave authenticity to the new.

Here is Short Bull, with a message to the Sioux shortly before
the battle of Wounded Knee:

> My friends and relations: I will soon start this thing [the millen-
> nium] in running order. I have told you that this would come to
> pass in two seasons, but since the whites are interfering so much, I
> will advance the time from what my father above told me to do,
> so the time will be shorter. Therefore, you must not be afraid of
> anything. Some of my relations have no ears, so I will have them
> blown away.
>
> Now there will be a tree sprout up, and there all the members
> of our religion and the tribe must gather together. That will be the
> place where we will see our dead relations. But before this time the
> earth will shiver very hard. Whenever this thing occurs, I will
> start the wind to blow. We are the ones who will then see our
> fathers, mothers, and everybody. We, the tribe of Indians, are the
> ones who are living a sacred life. God, our father himself, has told
> and commanded and shown me to do these things.
>
> My father has shown me these things, therefore we must con-
> tinue this dance [The Ghost Dance]. If the soldiers surround you
> four deep, three of you, *on whom I have put holy shirts* [supposedly
> bullet-proof], will sing a song, which I have taught you, around
> them, when some of them will drop dead. Then the rest will start
> to run, but their horses will sink into the earth. The riders will
> jump from their horses, but they will sink into the earth also.
> Then you can do as you desire with them. Now, you must know,
> this, that all the soldiers and that race [the whites] will be dead.
> There will be only five thousand of them living on the earth. . . .

[1] See *Hoebel* (1); (2), pp. 11–16; and *Ewers*, pp. 174–84, 298ff.

Now, we must gather at Pass Creek where the tree is sprouting.
There we will go among our dead relations. You must not take any
earthly things with you. Then the *men must take off all their
clothing and the women must do the same.* No one shall be ashamed
of exposing their persons. My father above has told us to do this, and
we must do as he says. You must not be afraid of anything. The
guns are the only things we are afraid of, but they belong to our
father in heaven. He will see that they do no harm. Whatever
white men may tell you, do not listen to them, my relations. That
is all. I will now raise my hand up to my father and close what he
has said to you through me.[1]

Is there not a note of desperation in that concluding 'whatever white men may tell you, do not listen to them, my relations'? Here were people the reverse of 'forgetful' but 'desolate
and in doubt' indeed—yet taking comfort in what a prophet had
to say, and who took action because of what a prophet had to
say. Perhaps one may be allowed to see the battle of Wounded
Knee not as the horror that in fact it was, but rather as a final
attempt to gain a traditional kind of redemption. For the battle
was not overtly intended by either side. Starting as an in-
augural for peace, during which the Sioux were to hand over
their arms, an excited young Indian, losing control and com-
posure in the tension accompanying the surrender, drew a rifle
from under his blanket and fired at the white soldiers who were
present in large numbers.[2] At this the whites too lost control,
and three hundred and seventy Indian men, women and children were killed in the massacre that followed.

Dead men can be replaced. But here it was traditional Plains
Indian culture itself which had been destroyed. The survivors
had to find quite new principles and assumptions on which to
base community life. Mere individuals with common traditions,
they had to reintegrate themselves as communities based on
quite different assumptions from those they had known in the
past. But, unlike the more usual desert island 'starting again',
there was little material on which they could exercise their
imaginations and traditional technical skills. First they had to
become an organized community. A prophet could say, more
positively, 'Do right always'. But what kinds of activities could

[1] *Mooney*, p. 31 (my italics. Cf. Mambu above, p. 65).
[2] *Mooney*, p. 118.

be thought of as 'right' now or in the future? Traditionally, the 'right' thing to do always was to stand one's ground, defend one's honour and integrity, and fight. Yet they were being told not to do precisely this. What was a 'right' thing to do—what the whites told them to do? Should they wait patiently in lodge or tipi doing no harm to anyone until a nervous Indian agent, afraid that his community might starve to death, handed out supplies from the trade store? Certainly they could plant a little tobacco. But few of these survivors knew how to grown corn or vegetables, or how to rear chickens and pigs so that there would be a 'right' way of doing it which, through the productive and distributive process, would demonstrate ability, prestige and integrity. Wage labour in the towns? That meant being controlled and treated as a 'naturally' inferior sort of person. With a future that could only be phrased in vague and general abstractions, it is hardly matter for surprise that such abstractions as might be realized, were in fact realized in terms of traditional activities. Those injunctions that could not be realized in terms of past activities could hardly be realized at all. As it was, those traditional activities which could be taken into the future—trance states, self-torture, the seeking of a guardian spirit by means of techniques calculated to induce a release from ordinary worldly and social cares, communication with the ancestors and so continuity with the cultural heritage —were contained within the rituals of the Ghost Dance itself. As in so many other instances over the world, the activity of the communal dance—in which participants might speak as with tongues, have visions, escape from the prisons of the body and formal modes of knowledge, gain inspiration—seems to have been the seed of such organizational forms as were to develop in the years that followed.

Faced with organizing themselves from virtually nothing into quite new kinds of communities, the Plains Indians could only realize new ways of behaving by using traditional sources of authority. That these traditional sources were sought through the communal dance and its accompanying trance-like states, takes the Plains Indians out of their purely cultural context and places them in a generally human setting.[1] For not only does the communal trance-dance appear as a generally human device

[1] Cf. *Burridge* (3), pp. 1–14.

for seeking inspiration and fresh initiatives, it is in itself the communal expression and analogue of just that experience whereby a prophet, a lone individual, comes to be inspired with the revelation that others afterwards discover they would like to make their own.

THE PAHARIAS AND ORAONS

The destruction of the buffalo herds of the North American plains was completed in about fifteen years. And though we can say that the destruction of Plains Indian culture started with the first whites who came onto the plains, this would be making too fine a point. While there were herds of buffalo Plains Indian culture was a going concern, a formidable antagonist to white armies and settlers. But when white hunters started killing the buffalo to feed a market for hides, Plains Indian culture was doomed. In fifteen years these people were reduced from their glories to almost nothing—a traumatic experience indeed. Yet this same process of destroying a people's integrity may be spread over several generations, nearly two centuries in the case about to be discussed, that of the Oraons of north-eastern India. But in both cases the result was the same. Some means of establishing an integrity fitted to a new total environment had to be found.

About two hundred years ago, the Oraons of Chota Nagpur were a congeries of non-Hindu peoples who, forming a confederation of polities, had elected a Rajah to represent them to the outside world.[1] To this Rajah they paid tax or tribute in kind and rendered certain customary services. In return they expected their Rajah to protect them from the outside world. But the Rajah and his immediate entourage became Hinduized, taking on Hindu ways. Indeed, if the Rajah was to maintain viable relations with the Hindu princelings on the peripheries of the lands owned by the Oraons he had to become Hinduized. Both he and his successors in office had to demonstrate to their neighbours the power and wealth befitting a Rajah. Hindu moneylenders and rentiers were invited in.

---

[1] Material taken from *Ekka*. Other sources: *Roy* (1) and (2); *Serrin*; *Fuchs*.

Gradually land started slipping out of the hands of the native villagers and into the grasp of the intruders. Now land was to the Oraon villagers as buffalo was to the Plains Indians. Land was inalienable, held in the lineage, a sacred trust from the first-comers and founders who had handed it on to their descendants. Oraons found their integrity in being landowners, found relative prestige among themselves by comparing the skill and industry with which households and lineages exploited the resources of land at their disposal. But cash had entered their economy. Successive Rajahs demanded higher and higher proportions of cash to kind. The moneylenders were the means of supplying the cash to the villagers. The villagers mortgaged their lands to the moneylenders in order to find the cash.

When the first European administrators and missionaries arrived in Chota Nagpur, the situation had already come near to breaking point. But though the administrators seem to have appreciated the situation quite accurately, they had only their own legal conventions to work with. Time and again they were forced to confirm the Hindu intruders in possession. Without deeds, without papers, not knowing how to write, the Oraons were helpless. They turned to the missionaries. They, warned by the administration that the situation was one of great tension, and that they (the missionaries) should only do what they could within the law as it stood, did their best. They advised the Oraons to keep calm and take legal steps. This they did. But the only lawyers whom they could employ—at some expense at that—were Hindus from Calcutta. These men used the opportunity to screw more and more money out of the Oraons whilst explaining the interminable delays of settlement by a succession of plausible stories. In the meantime, perhaps because they sensed that the missionaries were on their side, many Oraons became Christians. But as the years passed and the lawyers' stories became more and more imaginative, so the Oraons became poorer and poorer, more and more restive. At last, tiring of the lawyers and their delays, the Oraons began to take action. Lawyers' agents were beaten up. Disillusioned with the missionaries whose Christianity did not seem to be regaining their lands for them, large numbers seceded from the missions to join once-Christian prophets who had begun to preach direct action, new rites, new beliefs, new sets of assumptions.

Millenarian movements started and military action had to be taken by the administrative power.

Two hundred years of history and increasing tension have been compressed into this brief story. But they suffice to make the essential points: the entry of cash; the loss of lands on which integrity was built; recourse of missionaries and the Christian influence; the attempt to gain redress by legal procedures. Only after all else had failed did the Oraons attempt to transcend their difficulties by recourse to millenarian activities.

It is instructive to compare the lot of the Oraons with their neighbours, the Paharias, a people very similar to the Oraons but with a quite different history. While organized in much the same way as the Oraons, the Paharias had no Rajah. No Hindu moneylenders or rentiers entered their territories. They remained unmolested until the coming of European administrators. These administrators, finding a people pristine in their traditions, did little to change their traditional life and did nothing to impair their traditional forms of integrity. On the contrary, by accident or design they succeeded in making traditional forms of prestige even more prestigious. Village headmen were confirmed in office; native lands were reserved; cash entered in exchange for produce. If Hindu traders could take what to them was profit, Paharias were pleased with what to them was a bargain. Police and military forces were locally recruited, and those who served abroad returned as heroes with money. No millenarian activities took place among the Paharias.

Hindu colonization of the Oraons followed by European administration and Christian missionary influence give shape to the millenarian movements that actually occurred. But the cancer of wasting integrity went with money and land office registers. While some of the passionate desire to reassert one's integrity—so necessary to a millenarian movement—can be ascribed to the influence of the missionaries, we must also add that the Oraons had been made to appear small to themselves and unworthy of their heritage. The Paharias, on the other hand, were in their own eyes advanced in stature. Despite the arrival of European administrators such traditional ways as were vital to the integrity and pride of the people seem to have continued intact. Not only does the entry of money not seem to have impugned the traditional ways of measuring man and gaining prestige, it provided a spur to a wider redemptive process. There is no evidence of a competitive situation, no evidence that the different assumptions of administrators and Paharias competed or came into conflict over matters that were vital to either. A mutual tolerance that was hardly put to the test seems to have insulated one world from the other, and served to enable individuals to move between them without necessarily having to carry the concomitants of the one into the other. But would the case have been the same had the Paharias, or their administrators, been less content with themselves than they were?

THE JAINS

Their traditional expressions of integrity destroyed within the space of a generation, the Plains Indians of North America had to look backward in their attempts to move forward. And, because they are part of our own mythology, it is only too easy to see their gaze as frozen on the past to which they belong. Yet they have made a new man, wrought a new culture, found new ways. The integrity of the Oraons had been slowly eroded over several generations. But eventually, when the time seemed ripe, they asserted themselves. And they are still doing so. Through a mutual exclusion of the significant parts of two social orders, Paharias retained the substance of a traditional integrity. Now we turn to a quite different scene, the founding of Jainism.

The beginnings of Jainism is an apposite instance because, though distant both in space and time from the strict sense of the meaning of 'millenarian', it reveals on the one hand much the same patterns we have come to associate with activities labelled 'millenarian', and on the other hand it shows that in trying to analyse millenarian movements we are trying to conceptualize processes of beginnings. But if the relevances of Jainism are to be appreciated, we have to remember that the first Jains belonged to a highly sophisticated civilization. We are not here dealing with a simple or 'primitive' people. At the same time, we have to treat what seem to be the bare facts of the action in much the same way as we would treat the activities of a simpler people. Comparative sociology entails this kind of initial crudity.

The founding of Jainism is usually identified with the work of Mahavira the Jain, also known as Vardhamana, the increasing, or as Vaisaliya. A contemporary of Gautama Buddha (557–477 B.C.) Mahavira is said to have been born in 599 B.C. in Magadha in north India, dying in 527 B.C. at Pava, not far from the present Patna.[1] Both Gautama and Mahavira travelled over the same country. But if the dates are at all accurate, Mahavira was dead or dying when Gautama started his preaching. Nevertheless, there are close correspondences between the founding of Jainism and the founding of Buddhism, and there seems every likelihood that the same people who were involved in the early beginnings of Jainism were also involved in the early beginnings of Buddhism. And though some authors assert that Gautama and Mahavira were two different representations of the same prophet,[2] what is important to us here is that, whether as an individual or as a representation, Mahavira is acceptable as a precursor to Gautama. A pattern noticed earlier begins to assert itself.[3]

In the broadest terms the social organization of the peoples to whom both Gautama and Mahavira preached was determined by two categories of person, the Brahman and the Kshatriya. Both were literate and educated, and in each of them was vested, in different ways, the bulk of the power available to Hindu society at the time. The Brahman was scholar and priest, the sacerdotal academic. The Kshatriya was warrior and ruler, political boss and executive. For both these categories life, the state of being alive, or the activity of living, was thought of as a penance, a suffering, an undesirable finite imprisonment of souls in bodies. The final goal to be obtained, redemption, was the release of the soul from the bondage of finite life and absorption into the absolute all-being, *Brahma*

---

[1] Main sources used are *Stevenson*; *Jaini*; *Basham*.

[2] *Stevenson*, pp. 27–9.

[3] For example, Mambu and many other prophets were precursors of Yali (above, pp. 64–9); Te Kooti followed Te Ua (above, pp. 20–1); the *Kekesi* rites were followed by the *Baigona* cult, the *Taro* cult, and the *Vailala Madness* (above, pp. 53–5).

(neuter), a state or position known as *moksha* (release). However, not only was *moksha* dependent on certain observances which the Kshatriya, by virtue of his role in society, could hardly perform, but, as matter of axiom, only Brahmans had access to this release. In vulgar terms, though both categories stood on common ground in terms of their ideals and aspirations, only one of them could realize these aspirations and ideals and gain release.

Family and public ceremonials were accompanied by rituals, and good fortune and success depended on the rituals being properly performed. Improperly performed rituals were believed to result in misfortunes and even death. But only Brahmans could carry out these rituals, only Brahmans knew these rituals accurately. And while Brahmans performed these rituals for all twice-born castes, it was the Kshatriyas who employed them most, and who, as political leaders and rulers, crucially required that the rituals be performed correctly. Learning, writing and knowledge of the Vedas carried prestige throughout society. Together, they were a passport to lucrative positions at court, a source of wealth. But though Kshatriyas were educated, and shared in the learning of the Brahmans, they could never be as learned as the Brahmans if only because they had other duties to attend to. Then again, knowledge of the *mantras*— efficacious phrases whose pronouncements were thought to have a causal effect—was necessary to the carrying out of any endeavour. But while the Kshatriyas were the people who made the endeavours, who had administrative and political tasks to perform, the Brahmans had an exclusive knowledge of the *mantras* which alone gave the endeavours a chance of success.

Sacrifice, the focus in early days of both religious and social life, and the responsibility of the political leaders, the Kshatriyas, required a Brahman to officiate, and the goodwill of the Brahman if it was to be brought to a successful conclusion. In the days of the great horse sacrifice, for example, immense logistic and organizational skills were required to bring people, goods and produce together in a more or less orderly fashion. But if the Brahman was unwilling the effort and sacrifice were in vain. Again, though the laws of Manu do not emerge in finished form until very much later, they were a Brahmanical product, and they seem to indicate the relationship between Brahman and Kshatriya at this earlier period. A few excerpts are appropriate:

> To Brahmans HE (*Brahma*) assigned teaching and studying the Vedas, sacrificing for their own benefit and for others, the giving and accepting of alms.
> The Kshatriya HE commanded to protect the people, to bestow gifts, to offer sacrifices, to study the Vedas, and to abstain from attaching himself to sensual pleasures.
> The Vaishya to tend cattle, to bestow gifts, to offer sacrifices, to study the Vedas, to trade, to lend money, and to cultivate land.
> One occupation only the Lord prescribed to the Sudra: to serve meekly the other three castes. . . .[1]
> A Brahman coming into existence, is born as the highest on earth, the Lord of all created beings, for the protection of the treasury of the law.
> Whatever exists in the world is the property of the Brahman; on account of the excellence of his origin, the Brahman is, indeed, entitled to it all.
> The Brahman eats his own food, wears his own apparel, bestows but his own alms; other mortals subsist through the benevolence of the Brahman.
> Know that a Brahman of ten years and a Kshatriya of a hundred years stand to each other in the relation of father and son; but between those two the Brahman is the father.
> A Brahman, be he ignorant or learned, is a great divinity. Though Brahmans employ themselves in all sorts of mean occupations, they must be honoured in every way. For each is a great deity. . . .[2]

The excerpts show in a formal way the status of Brahman to Kshatriya. And they also show, again in a formal way, the degree to which they had managed to control the society they lived in. On the other hand, there were also many injunctions exhorting Brahman and Kshatriya to co-operate. For although a Brahman was as a god on earth, and the earth was said actually to belong to him, Kshatriyas were allowed to rule it so that Brahmans could avoid the taking of life and might devote themselves to ritual and learning. And taking life, one of the primary and fundamental barriers to *moksha*, is often a political necessity—even where it is merely executing a criminal or a murderer.

[1] Manu I 89–91.   [2] Manu I 99–102.

> When the world was without a King and
> dispersed in fear in all directions
> The Lord created a King for the protection
> of all.[1]
> If the King did not inflict punishment
> unerringly on evildoers the
> stronger would roast the weaker
> like fish upon a spit. . . .[2]

The King and his aides were Kshatriyas.

Within the relationship Brahman-Kshatriya, then, the Brahmans arrogated to themselves exclusive access to that release, *moksha*, which brought an end to the successive transmigrations of the soul, and its successive involvements in bodily form, in life as lived on earth. While the Brahmans, normally protected from the vicissitudes of life, were well placed to earn their release, the Kshatriyas, sharing the self-same ideals and aspirations, but as rulers and political leaders inevitably involved in worldly affairs, open to many temptations and in the position more often than not of having to choose between two evils, were impossibly placed. They could not gain access to *moksha*. So that, given these relations between Brahman and Kshatriya, it will not come as a surprise to learn that before either Mahavira or Gautama appeared on the scene they had been preceded by a series of other prophets or teachers who, mostly drawn from the Kshatriya category, had rejected the main tenets of the Brahmanical scheme. There were materialists who held that, apart from the body and other concrete things, there was no other existence. One lived, one died, one was burnt, and in the course of time the particulars of being became reintegrated into some other thing or body. There were fatalists who held that it mattered nothing what one did in life, whether one was virtuous or thieved, gave alms, committed adultery or murder. All was preordained, foreseen, unchangeable. Men and women simply had to act out the parts which had been prescribed for them. In one way or another these teachers or prophets attacked Brahmanical exclusivism and particular facets of the three-pillared scheme to which it was related; *karma*, works and doing; *samsara*, the wandering and trans-

[1] Manu VII 3–5.   [2] Manu VII 39.

migration of souls; and *moksha*, release from *karma* and *samsara* to become absorbed in the absolute All-being.

The significance of these precursors may be appreciated on several levels. Historically, we can see Mahavira and Gautama as end-points in a developing ferment of ideas which were challenging orthodox assumptions and positing new ones. And as end-points in a flux of ideas Mahavira and Gautama launch forth into certainty with the beginnings of Jainism and Buddhism. Flux has become three kinds of formal certainty: traditional Hinduism or Brahmanism; Jainism; and Buddhism. On the level of myth, since both in Jainism and Buddhism the innovating creators, Mahavira and Gautama, are considered to have had precursors who are not historically identifiable, we can appreciate the representation of that probing back into traditional sources which we have remarked as being characteristic of the prophet. Neither Mahavira nor Gautama arrived full-grown. They emerged from the historical past, have been given a mythical or doctrinal past, and are represented as having emerged from traditional sources of authority. The accolade of authenticity demands continuity with the past, with traditional sources of authority.

Bearing in mind the Judaeo-Christian tradition of successive prophets, and accepting that both Mahavira and Gautama had historical precursors who dealt with much the same problems as they did themselves, we may well ask whether the relationship between Brahman and Kshatriya is such that between them they must generate the *guru*, teacher or prophet. If so, then it is surely a basic relationship which is by its nature a developmental process also. We ought to examine it more closely.

We may make a start with the prophet. What is he to do when once he has been generated? First, though he might appear to want to formulate something new, and may even believe that he is doing just this, he cannot himself think at all except in traditional terms, he cannot communicate with his audience unless he uses the concepts and ideas that are already familiar to them. He is forced to use traditional sources. Second, because he has to use traditional ideas to formulate the new, however radical the thought of a teacher might be or be thought by himself or others to be, in after years it is bound to look like some kind of synthesis. Even where a form of syncretism is farthest from the thoughts of an innovator, in the years to come his work assumes the form of a synthesis. It cannot appear as anything else. Not only is authenticity born of tradition, but an acceptable prophet is an innovator who synthesizes, not simply an innovator.

Let us now look at what seems to have been the situation in north India when Mahavira and Gautama started to teach. It was a period of theological troubles certainly, as the successive teachers or prophets bear witness. But it was also a time of economic adjustments. Numbers of virtually or nominally independent city states, headed by rajahs or princes and confederated or allied or in a variety of types of suzerainty, had been developing fairly rapidly. And since trade, too, between the several principalities was very much on the increase, one may assume the emergence of a mercantile class who managed this trade. Not themselves necessarily engaged in processes of manufacture, but managing, capitalizing and financing this trade, such a class would tend to employ the managerial techniques of the Kshatriyas. But, though wealthy and powerful, they would not be warriors or hold political office. They would be struggling to fit themselves into a social order in which, theoretically or theologically, they had no place. And if we cast forward a few years we find that the Jains were to become precisely this class of financiers and managers of trade. That is, appreciating the economic role of Jainism, we can see that when Mahavira appeared Hindu society was, as it were, beckoning the Jains into existence.

It is often thought that both Jainism and Buddhism were particular reactions to the caste system, the social projection of Hinduism. Stevenson refines this view to point out that Jainism was not so much a reaction to the caste system as a reaction against the Brahmans and their claim to an exclusive access to *moksha*. Indeed, the later history of Jainism confirms the point. For there is little or no evidence to show that Jainism contained any objection to the caste system. All along Jains have been involved in the caste system; all along they have employed Brahman chaplains. So that though the Jains, initially drawn from the Kshatriya category, might, in virtue of the Brahman-Kshatriya relationship, be thought to be reacting against the Brahmans themselves, the evidence shows otherwise.

What then were the Jains reacting against? On one level, clearly, the break between Jainism and orthodox Hinduism turns on a theological point: that given an adherence to certain observances, *moksha* was available to all and not just to Brahmans. Mahavira accepted the principles of orthodox Hinduism; he accepted the implications of the three pillars of *karma*, *samsara* and *moksha*. But he rejected the exclusive prerogative of the Brahmans to obtain release from the cycle of rebirths and bodily imprisonments. *Moksha*, he said, was open to anyone who could achieve it. There is, here, a partial antagonism towards the Brahmans but, and much more significantly, a revulsion on the part of Kshatriyas against continuing to be Kshatriyas. Mahavira did not contest the hierarchy of shared values. What he did contest, as a Kshatriya himself, was that Kshatriyas should be debarred from the benefits of those values. The principle of *moksha* itself was not in question. If anything, Mahavira insisted on a harder course. What he set himself against was the fact that Kshatriyas, by virtue of their role in society, were virtually debarred from gaining access to *moksha*.

Stevenson lists three paradoxes to be found in Jainism.[1] First, Jainism originated among Kshatriyas, warriors, but the central tenet of Jainism, also held by the Brahmans, was *ahimsa*, the aversion to killing or wounding any form of life. Second, though the founders of Jainism were aristocrats, Jainism gained acceptance by the middle mercantile class, and Jains were to become a mercantile class. Third, Jain unworldliness, the giving up of wealth, is combined with the fact that Jains are, and always have been, extremely wealthy people. For centuries they were the bankers of India. Now encouraged and supported by rajahs whom they, the Jains, supported, now persecuted by those other princes whom the Jains thought a bad investment, the history of Jainism goes together with a history of financial management in India.

Just how paradoxical are these features of Jainism? If Jainism is regarded not so much as a revolt against caste or the Brahmans, but as a revulsion on the part of Kshatriyas against continuing to be Kshatriyas, then these paradoxical or contrary features of Jainism resolve themselves. Being aristocratic political leaders and warriors debars them from *moksha*. Therefore

[1] *Stevenson*, pp. 7–8.

Kshatriyas must become something else. Familiar with the techniques of organization, they become merchants and entrepreneurial managers, controlling the finance on which trade depends. If renunciation of possessions is to have any meaning, there must be possessions to renounce. Unlike the Shakers of North America, whose requirements for a community life based upon renunciation of all possessions was met by recruitment from outside—the new recruit donating all he had to the community treasure chest—and the prohibition of sexual relations and marriage between themselves,[1] Jains fulfilled and generated themselves as an organized community by a precise definition of marriage accompanied by the accumulation of wealth and possessions, followed by individual renunciations of possessions. This made them into a viable group and also enabled individuals to make their essential renunciation.

Jains divide themselves into two main sections, monks and mendicants on the one hand, and laymen on the other. The layman accumulates possessions, and then renounces them to become a monk or mendicant. While the life of a monk or mendicant is free from worldly involvement, devoted entirely to spiritual contemplation, the layman's life is tabulated and arranged with mathematical precision. Involvement in worldly affairs is accurately measured.[2] From childhood on the layman has before him a successive series of exercises and tests which he should undergo. Quantitatively conceptualized in terms of amounts, distances, and periods of time, exercises and tests are directly related to *ahimsa* and the dissipation of *karma* in order to obtain release or *moksha*. They are designed to bring the human passions and desires under control. Gradually becoming more and more severe, they allow a Jain to involve himself in the affairs of the counting house until, reaching middle age, he becomes wealthy, has stature, and is as neutral to passion and desire as the money he handles. Then, reaching an apogee, further successive exercises and degrees disbar him from involvement as they become more and more restrictive in relation to diet, spatial movement, muscular activity, and sexual life. Eventually, wholly insulated from worldly affairs, with desires and bodily activities ground to a minimum, he becomes a

[1] *Andrews.*   [2] *Stevenson,* pp. 193–250.

mendicant or monk, dependent for food and shelter on those Jains who are still involved in affairs.

Of all the activities that might be thought suitable to the ideals and aspirations of Jainism, surely none could be more appropriate than the management of money. No other group has so finely systematized and married the qualitative and quantitative measures of man. Dominated by Number and Quantity, the amount of *karma* to be excised, money accurately and concretely measures the preferred and selected qualities until the time comes when, disburdened and without money, the spiritual qualities are referred to the abstract idea of number itself.

The fact that Jainism has never spread outside its Indian or Hindu context to any great extent shows, perhaps, the very narrow and specialized theological point in dispute. The conditions of being for a Jain remain closely related to a particular theology or set of assumptions which, in European eyes, are as empty of heart and passion as the coins which measure their behavioural projection. In the beginning, however, the passion was there, and the founders of Jainism trod a universal pattern. The moment we step outside the labels 'Brahman' and 'Kshatriya' we enter into a figured logic of relations with analogues everywhere: where two groups or categories of persons share the same values or assumptions, but only one of these groups or categories has access to the rewards or benefits implied in the shared values, then the *guru* or prophet is generated, new assumptions enter the arena, a new group or category of persons may come into being. The fact that Mahavira himself, as well as his immediate followers, the founders, were sprung from those who did not wish to remain themselves but wanted to be something other, also has a universal relevance. It enables us to appreciate on the level of action how a conflict—Haddon's 'oppression'—need not be outer-directed but may be inner-directed. The inner turmoil of heart and mind must be externalized. Finally, because Jainism is removed from our own millennial traditions, we can appreciate how far and in what senses millenarian activities are not necessarily correlated with a colonial situation as such. For where millenarian activities have occurred within the context of a long-established theological and historical tradition, while the overtly important points at issue appear as theological, turning on basic assumptions about man's condition, these in their turn relate to integrity and the ways in which a particular kind of redemption may be won.

If 'integrity' seems a vague term, cheapened by careless usage, it retains a core of meaning and, as has been shown, can be broken down into propositions susceptible of empirical investigation. For the Maori of the Waikato integrity—in which is subsumed relative standing and prestige—and so redemption were to be found primarily in particular approaches to given relations between land, *mana*, and warfare. Though in all cases other skills and qualities must play their parts, the same kinds of selected dominant relations can be seen among the Melanesians in relation to the effective deployment of produce and artifacts; among the Plains Indians in relation to physical courage, warfare, stealing horses and hunting buffalo; among the Oraons in relation to their attachment to a hereditary right to particular parcels of land; among the Jains in relation to their insistence that all men have a right to redemption through *moksha*. Many more instances could be cited; the range and variety of cultural and theological expressions are legion. Qualities of integrity are contained within, and emerge from, the redemptive process. They are secreted in the modes of exploitation of material resources, in the ways in which such exploitation is accorded approval, esteem, influence and power; they are demonstrated by prescribed behaviour in selected areas and arenas of social life. When integrity is ill-defined, or unattainable, qualities of conscience—upon which a moral order ultimately depends—become correspondingly vitiated and random. When this happens the bases of power become random and unordered. When assumptions about power are in doubt, when the redemptive process is in doubt, when the prestige system is in doubt, then integrity is in doubt. And when integrity is in doubt, a new man—born of new assumptions, a new redemptive process, and a new prestige system—becomes necessary. The price is spiritual and moral covetousness.

8

Problems of Classification

Having sketched out the general nature of millenarian activities, seen what they are like by means of a few selected examples, and posed some problems of conceptualization and analysis, we can now turn to ask how we may distinguish one kind of millenarian movement from another. First, however, let us again take stock. Within

(i) a generally permissive political regime, there may arise

(ii) competing sets of assumptions about power which relate to particular kinds of prestige and integrity, and so to redemption. Particularly is this so when

(iii) participating in or sharing the self-same hierarchy of values and aspirations, one of two groups or categories within the whole is underprivileged in that it has no access to the kind of redemption which the shared aspirations and values imply. Yet even if there appears to be a conflict between one group or category and another

(iv) the outer-directed antagonism may be subsidiary to an inner-directed antagonism on the part of one group or category which, in preferring not to continue to be itself, aspires to be something other. Since too

(v) integrity and prestige emerge from particular kinds of measurement of man, money, a quantitative and fac-torial measure, has decisive significance in relation to traditionally qualitative measures within a system of binary opposites. In all cases, however

(vi) new beginnings are predicated, a new kind of community is in genesis.

(vii) In order to realize these new beginnings and give form and order to the new community, traditional sources of authority are tapped and rechannelled. Initially

(viii) there may be no prophet: in which case the new assumptions may be regarded as implicit rather than explicit. But if these castings about in search of a point of departure are to develop into something more coherent there must come

(ix) a prophet or teacher who, usually having precursors, articulates the new assumptions of the emergent new community, brings direction and certainty to a situation characterized by uncertainty and no direction. Usually

(x) a trance-dance, a device which echoes the experience of the prophet himself, and whereby the new insights into traditional sources of authority may be gained, accompanies first beginnings and may continue as a more formally developed ritual.

(xi) New assumptions are expressed within the terms of a particular cultural idiom. And while

(xii) the historical background to a particular set of activities, and the precursors of a prophet, provide an investigator with insights into the cultural idiom, and help him understand why the activities take the form they do, nevertheless

(xiii) each set of activities, each movement, is in itself self-justifying. If they were not self-justifying there would be an invariable relation between the conditions obtaining and the occurrence of a movement. But we do not find this. On the other hand, working within terms of probabilities and possibilities, we find that these activities, when they occur, are not simply existential, but relate to

(xiv) the making of a new man who is born of the new assumptions which, developing within an historical continuum, guarantee the new redemption.

(xv) Hence the recurrence of series of millenarian activities within the context of a particular cultural and historical tradition.

(xvi) Though many millenarian movements and activities are preceded by purely political or even legal measures, these turn out to be partial solutions to a series of problems which

(xvii) the succeeding millenarian activities purport to transcend in their entirety. How far the activities succeed or fail in attaining the overt objectives

(xviii) cannot be judged within the narrow context of the initial activities themselves. They are to be appreciated on a much longer time scale, within an historical continuum, in terms of first beginnings and further and ultimate consequences. It may then become clearer how and in what sense

(xix) the encompassing social order in which the activities take place may seem to have been, as it were, awaiting or demanding just such a community as has come into existence.[1]

The summary above poses the question whether, given such a general framework, there are any logical distinctions between one kind of movement and another. That the distinctions should refer to the logic of social relations rather than to the empirical reality is of some importance. For since every set of activities must be empirically different from another, each movement becomes a class on its own. Unless we examine the logical patterns no kind of classification is possible. Even the fact that each movement is self-justifying and is not necessarily explicable in terms of the wider context of social relations, does not vitiate the injunction that our proper concern is with sets, types or patterns of social relations however these may be contingently or culturally expressed.

So far as the activities we have been describing are not contained within a Judaeo-Christian ambience, or are not contained within a sustained and written tradition that there will come a man, sent from God or the divine, who will deliver or redeem his people, they are quite incorrectly described as millenarian, messianic, or chiliastic. Yet this is surely the very kind of ethnocentric nominalism we should avoid. Because all the activities we have in mind envisage some kind of redemption, some kind of release from current obligations through an inspiration regarded locally as divine, it seems sensible to think of them as generally millenarian. Because, as we shall see,[2] all these activities and movements envisage redemption itself, a

[1] Compare *Fuchs*, p. 1, where a similar kind of formulation is yet significantly different.

[2] Below, pp. 165–70.

condition of being which is without rules, without obligations,[1] but also envisage a condition in which new rules will provide the framework of a fuller and more wholesome redemptive process, they are more usefully thought of as millenarian even though there is no messiah as such. Should we then distinguish between movements that take place within a tradition which looks forward to a coming redeemer or prophet from those which lack such a tradition? There are difficulties here. For with the first prophet in a region a 'tradition' is established. If we distinguish between written and oral traditions, what are to say of Te Ua and other Maori who were literate and reasonably familiar with Revelations in a generally non-literate environment? How long must a 'tradition' be established before it becomes a 'true' tradition? On the whole the distinction does not seem to be useful except perhaps in marginal cases.

Classification by reference to geographical region and historical period is sometimes useful in that it provides rough co-ordinates which enable us to predict with some slight assurance what form a movement might take. We can talk about the Enthusiastic movements of the seventeenth and eighteenth centuries,[2] or about cargo cults as being typical of Melanesia. We can go even further and distinguish cargo cults from other movements in that an uninhibited and unrestricted access to material goods is a feature of the millennium. Yet so soon as we begin to think about these material goods and what they symbolize, the distinction begins to lose force. It is not analytically useful to distinguish cargo cults from buffalo cults and land cults or money cults and so on. Nor do we gain much by thinking of enthusiastic movements as in some way essentially sociologically distinct from medieval or nineteenth century millenarianisms, just because they occurred in different periods of time. Precisely this kind of distinction is what a sociologist seeks to overcome. But again, as an *ad hoc* distinction, by qualifying 'activities' or 'cult' or 'movement' by 'cargo' or 'enthusiastic' we get an idea of what is in view.

Can we find useful distinctions within the general class of activity prefaced by 'cargo'? We can at once perceive that within a wide area of common ground there are differences of emphasis, and that the role of the prophet is not always pre-

---

[1] Above, p. 6.　　　　　　[2] See *Knox*.

cisely the same. On the first point, however, as soon as we go into detail, these differences of emphasis begin to disappear and become entirely subjective. Even if we think of 'emphasis' as connoting a set of relations, the envisaging, for example, of particular kinds of relations between white men and black, or between the administration and others, there still emerges no classification that is useful in other contexts. Some cargo movements are quite evidently related to a central myth, while in others the myth does not seem to be so important. Yet it would be foolish to say that because no myth had been reported here was a criterion of distinction. On the evidence, indeed, one would be better advised to assume the existence of a myth and then look for it. What some call myth others call 'doctrine', and few of the basic assumptions of a community are not figured in myth.

The role of the prophet seems a much more promising line of attack, for we can, in the first instance, distinguish the episodes where no prophet appears from activities in which a prophet plays a central part. Clearly, few of the prophets of Oceania, America, Africa and most parts of Asia rise to the standards set by the prophets of the Old Testament. Rarely do they claim to speak for the one and all-powerful God, nor do we find any traditions that they should do. Spirit possession does not meet the requirements of prophetism. *Ad hoc*, without continuity in a literate tradition, rarely do those possessed by spirits claim to utter universal truths derived from the source of All Truth. On the other hand, the central figures or leaders of millenarian movements are certainly prophets. They articulate what they believe to be truths, and they derive these truths from what is taken to be a divine inspiration. They speak of redemption, they have definite instructions on how this redemption is to be won and they speak to the community at large. If we consider Te Ua, Siovili, the old women of Samoa and the Cook Islands, Bia, Mambu, Yali, Ndungumoi and Mahavira it is clear, on the face of it, that we are dealing with several quite different kinds of prophet. But it is difficult to see how the more obvious differences in degrees of political awareness, range of influence, theological and intellectual sophistication, and type of vocation[1] predicate millenarian activities of different kinds. Given that,

[1] Cf. *Emmett.*

whatever the actual conditions of the time when he lived, Mahavira's precursors now imply at least a retrospective expectancy, he differs from, say, Bia, who was not expected and is not now taken to have been expected. But if Bia did not himself sustain a movement of any lasting consequence, was it Mahavira, his disciples, or their successors who put Jainism on its feet? And may not Bia be regarded as a precursor for the *Taro, Baigona* and *Vailala* activities? How long do we have to wait before we can use this kind of criterion in any particular instance? We cannot but evaluate Yali, say, in terms of what we know about Bia and Mambu; or Te Ua in terms of what we know about Siovili and Ndungumoi; or Mahavira in terms of what we know about Gautama or Mohammed or Kabir or James Naylor and a host of other prophets. By doing so we admit to differences between them, and we can make valid distinctions between the roles and attributes of particular prophets. Yet it is difficult to see how these differences mark out some movements as having different patterns of relations from others.

We might label some of these movements 'nativistic'[1]—meaning by this movements which, in rejecting European values advocate a return to traditional ways—and distinguish them from 'syncretic'[2] activities, in which both European and traditional elements are combined. But if we ask ourselves whether any millenarian movement is not nativistic in the sense that they do not adopt new ways—which must be taken from somewhere—we are back in the *cul de sac* of relative emphases. No simple community, once exposed to a wider culture, can do otherwise than attempt to make use of the ideas and artifacts that now come within reach. It is difficult to see how new assumptions can be realized anywhere other than by refurbishing selected traditional values. Nevertheless, both 'nativistic' and 'syncretic' are useful if impressionistic and subjective characterizations of particular aspects of the kinds of activities we have been discussing. But they are nothing more. Consider some of the better known descriptive terms which have been suggested as having analytical value: 'adjustment',[3] 'accom-

---

[1] *Linton.*
[2] *Lawrence* (1) and (2).
[3] *Piddington*, pp. 735–44; *Berndt* (3).

modative',[1] 'militant',[2] 'denunciatory',[3] 'revitalization',[4] 'vitalistic',[5] 'dynamic',[6] and 'reformative',[7] among others. Can we say that these descriptive terms, which refer to particular emphases as the investigators saw them, also refer to types of activities that are mutually exclusive? If for example we were to call the *Pai-marire* movement a militant movement, is there any good reason why we should not also call it a reformative or dynamic or vitalistic or denunciatory or accommodative movement? It was all of these things, and the choice between one term rather than another can only be subjective and confusing unless there is a consensus that, for convenience, we use one term rather than the others. Smith has suggested[8] that our view of millenarian activities should be restricted to *cult movements* (*sic*) which are (a) deliberate, conscious and organized; and (b) responses to social and economic dissatisfactions. This begs a host of questions and limits the enquiry to that which is overt. It excludes what seems to be the heart of the matter: assumptions about power, the impact of the prophet and his revelation, and the positive attempt to create a new man. On the other hand, Smith's further suggestions that we take into account certain stresses[9] (my 'relative emphases') in conjunction with particular contextual features,[10] while useful for *ad hoc* purposes is open to the criticism of subjective characterization and does not necessarily connote those sets of logical concomitants which are the essence of the problem of classification.

The nub of the matter may be restated in a different way. First, lacking a specific theory, or conceptual framework, such events as are observed can only be related to each other in ways which are wholly dependent on the investigator's intuitive insights. This has resulted in the series of eclectic empiricisms with which we are presently burdened. We ourselves surely need

---

[1] *Voget*; *Worsley*.   [2] *Smith* (2).   [3] *Barnett*.

[4] This term, suggested by *Wallace*, now has permanence in *Gould and Kolb*.

[5] *Linton*; *Wallace*; *Smith* (2).   [6] *Voget*.   [7] *Smith* (2); *Voget*.

[8] *Smith* (2).

[9] *Smith* (2): '*Nativism* stresses revived or perpetuated aspects of culture, *vitalism* stresses newly perceived aspects of culture, and *synthetism* stresses new combinations.' (Smith's italics.)

[10] Smith's contextual features (2) are: *messianic, millenarian, revivalistic, militant,* and *reformative.* (Smith's italics.)

a millenarian movement to give these views an overall coherence. Classification, the identification of significant similarities, distinctions and differences, can only emerge from an explanatory model which relates one kind of relationship to others in particular ways. And we shall presently discuss such models. Second, what is common to all millenarian movements is that series of related activities which we have summed up as the redemptive process. Hence it is the different kinds of redemptive process that we must eventually consider. Third, since all millenarian movements imply new beginnings, the remoulding of tradition into something new, they must eventually assume the form of syntheses between old and new. So, distinctions within the general class 'millenarian' are properly referred to different kinds of syntheses. And these last should, in turn, summarize the relations between the activities subsumed in the phrase 'a new redemptive process'. What anthropology cannot do, because it lacks the tools, is make a more than arbitrary decision on the spirituality of a millenarian movement. Yet it is precisely on this point that millenarists should wish to be judged.

9

General Pattern

In discussing the general nature of millenarian movements we have talked about sets of social relations. The illustrations have shown us how these relations may be expressed in terms of behaviour. Now we turn to the pattern of events which express these relations. The time-scale cannot be absolute; it must be regarded as flexible. Nor can the chronology be absolute. What we need is a general statement which will help us order the events of a particular movement. We have concentrated more directly on the colonial situation, the encounter between civilized literate and moneyed peoples, and the simpler peoples with a subsistence economy. But the pattern also seems to hold good for those movements that have occurred within the ambience of a civilized tradition.

We may think of this pattern as contained within three phases:

Phase 1

As the discussion on the *Kekesi* rites has shown,[1] this first phase may be characterized as an awareness of being disenfranchized. Separated from the mainstream of power and its associated activities, members of a community become, if only temporarily and for short periods, more and more aware of themselves as individuals. Having experienced what appears to them as a series of unique encounters, the content of shared experience begins to dwindle and men and women are forced back onto their own personal resources. Gradually, however, through conversation, gossip, anecdote and listening to rumours, the series of discrete and unique encounters begins to dissolve into a shared experience. And as numbers of lone individuals begin to become aware of their newly found common ground, so

[1] Above, pp. 53–5.

they begin more and more to associate, to become aware of themselves as enjoying a new kind of social being. At this point they are ready to enter the second phase.

First, however, let us break down the general statement above. A developing social order will call for the performance of new kinds of tasks, and here and there individuals will begin undertaking them. But in doing so they isolate themselves from an established and still relevant prestige system. They separate themselves from the institutions and procedures through which their worth may gain recognition; they distance themselves from the acknowledged means of redemption. So, to find recognition and a new mode of redemption, those who undertake the new tasks search into their traditions in order to find there those fundamental principles concerning redemption of which the traditional activities are but one expression. The traditional assumptions have to be so respun that the new tasks become a direct expression of them; and the ordering of the new tasks has to be brought into line with the new assumptions. Again and again within the Christian ambience, for example, as individuals have found themselves isolated from the mainstream of development, activities and power, so have they resorted to the scriptures to quarry for those principles of action which they considered most relevant to their extant condition. The same pattern is repeated in other civilizations. In the colonial situation, however, there is usually no book to resort to. The first encounter with the more sophisticated civilization produces a mixture of doubt, anxiety and hopeful expectation, a condition which may last for days, weeks, or years. There is much rumour-mongering, many discussions. Anecdotes are told. Perhaps the strangers will go as suddenly as they came, leaving tradition to resume its interrupted flow. But so soon as it becomes evident that the strangers have come to stay, first one individual, then another, becomes aware that his initiatives are his own, affecting nobody. One part of a man responds as an automaton; the other is engaged in experiencing and envisaging situations which can be neither controlled nor resolved satisfactorily. Bereft even of the illusion that they can command their own fates, the individuals who are coming into association also become aware that they are not doing the things they used to do. They ponder the question and search into the only universe of knowledge available; their own tradition. Sometimes this has the effect of reasserting traditional ways—a retreat into 'nativism'. Temporarily, perhaps, the fact of exclusion from the mainstream of power is obscured. Inevitably, however, the new ways demand their due. Then comes the attempt to understand the assumptions with which the new ways are associated. From explaining themselves and the strangers to themselves in terms of traditional assumptions, the simpler people begin to explain the same things in terms that represent a synthesis of the competing sets of assumptions.

This first phase is a ferment of intellectual endeavour, whether naïve or more sophisticated, and it is coloured by the strong emotions which accompany the awareness of severance. It is essentially an attempt to explain and comprehend the fact of disenfranchisement. People are unable to participate in or manipulate that power whose ordering connotes a higher or more satisfactory redemption. They begin to regard themselves as 'just rubbish' or as 'rubbish-men',[1] or feel they are regarded as such by others. But this cannot be borne. There must be some way of gaining an acknowledged integrity. Old myths and assumptions, whether handed down in an oral tradition or written down in authoritative form, tend to be construed anew. What the heart and stomach cannot passively accept, the mind's desire leaps forward to command. Aware of what might be, impotence swells with what might become potent. Yet this impulse to join the mainstream of power, to find a new integrity, does not necessarily imply being at the centre of the interactions of social life. For though the sectarian elect necessarily stand aside from the hub of established social life, they believe themselves to be more at one with that source of all power which the members of the wider society are also taken to acknowledge. What matters is that power, once recognized, should be ordered and rendered intelligible and that integrity should derive from this ordering.

Phase 2

The second phase is a testing of the tentative conclusions reached in the first phase. It is an attempt to give overt and

[1] The particular term 'rubbish-men' is taken from the Melanesian idiom.

active expression to the problems and their solutions; an attempt, through activity and the externalization of problems and solutions hitherto kept nearer the heart, to find and realize the new man; an attempt to transcend the dilemma of dissonances between competing assumptions. Necessarily syncretic, the new assumptions may have to reject parts of both sets of traditions in order to make the synthesis. Searching into the roots of Hinduism, the Jains rejected Brahman exclusiveness but accepted with more vehemence the principles by which *moksha* might be gained. Rejecting an organized priesthood and the sacramental life administered by priests, Christian enthusiasts went back to pentecostal traditions in order to realize what they believed was the essence of the Christian life. Taking Revelations and the angel Gabriel as his guide, Te Ua attempted to refashion his people's traditional symbols of power. The individuals who have come into association through their awareness of a common experience begin to express and communicate their new-found assumptions through the material and concrete, in activities. And through their activities they become more self-consciously aware of what their assumptions really are, what kinds of integrity they seek.

The activities usually centre about an economic issue, which focuses and gives momentum to the developing movement. Indeed, until individuals find common ground in concrete issues, their activities remain disorganized. The incidents on Manam Island provide an example. If the economic issue comes to a head before people have become aware of the fundamental assumptions involved, then it is likely that a purely politico-economic movement will develop. Usually, however, because the purely politico-economic solution cannot reach down to basic assumptions, it fails. Besides, an accommodation may be impossible because one side is too strong. What seems a political 'solution' merely reaffirms the fact of severance. Either way, if the activities are to develop into a millenarian movement they must transcend the politico-economic issues. For while lone individuals may associate for purely political or economic ends, they cannot participate in a millenarian movement unless they also aspire to transcend the purely politico-economic problems. On the one hand disorganized activities may be seen as the temporary aberrations of the severed and discontented, on the other hand they become informed with meaning and significance. The appearance in parts of New Guinea, for example, of flowers in vases, could not by themselves excite much comment. But given the millenarian ambience the flowers acquire a significance which not only expresses mundane political and economic issues but also transcends them. Opposition towards those in authority always has political and economic significance. But in a millenarian ambience satisfying purely political and economic aspirations will not suffice.

The kinds of issue which acquire a more than ordinary significance are clearly those which concern integrity. They refer to measures of man, to those ways of exploiting material resources which will demonstrate moral qualities and yield prestige and status. We may select for discussion four significant kinds of activity which are primary measures of man: industriousness; capacities of intellect; war making; and the handling of money. Let us take them in order.

Industriousness, hard work in one or a number of locally prescribed activities, is everywhere expected to carry a reward which is not merely the product of the activity itself. The industrious buffalo hunter among the Plains Indians ate no more meat than his fellows. But he reaped a reward in admiration which gave him prestige, influence and power within the community. Similarly, the hard-working cultivator, herdsman, artisan, entrepreneur or artist expects to earn the same kind of indirect reward either here on earth or in some heaven. When qualities of intellect, skill, cunning and shrewdness are added to industry, the hard-working man or woman is well positioned to exercise influence and power. But as prestige increases and influence widens, so obligations become more numerous and more difficult to handle. The redemptive process becomes more difficult, a higher or more worthy redemption is indicated. Yet capacities of intellect are also qualities in themselves. Their rewards are contained in some other state or activity. Whether as scholar or seer or story-teller or myth-maker, or as jester, wit or local savant in whatever field of endeavour, these capacities entitle the expert to an esteem beyond the confines of his field of competence. A sorcerer may gain command and make himself feared. A scholar earns more generalized respect. An artist has command over more than paint, stone, or rhythms. A seer,

shaman or holy man, however self-concerned, is required to
serve the community in political ways. And when these skills of
mind are appropriately brought to bear on such other tasks as
the community has to offer, again redemption is made more
difficult, a higher target is set. Industriousness and capacities
of mind clearly play their parts in war-making. But the latter
is essentially an activity in itself which measures the courageous
against the cowardly. Yet, given the political rewards of success,
qualities of courage and cowardliness reap a reward that continues beyond the encounter itself; they live on in myth, story,
history and tradition.

Logically separable, but intertwined in actual situations,
industry, capacities of mind, and war-making measure man
against man and distinguish him from the animal world. They
are qualitative criteria. One supreme act of courage outshines a
myriad ordinary braveries and cancels many examples of
cowardliness. The singular act of a particular man or woman
raises the status of all who are human. Such honour as is
accorded to scholars, teachers and mystics is earned only in so
far as it reflects the highest achievements of which the human
mind is capable. The ant and the bee work as industriously as
man, but neither bee nor ant seem to have much choice in the
matter. A man can opt out, deny himself, become something
less than a man; or he can show his quality.

Money may obscure these primary measures. It always
remains wealth, it always gives power. While it can reveal
qualities of industry, intellect and courage, it may also maintain sloth, ignorance and cowardice in power. Money may
negate those qualities of man generally regarded as deserving
merit, influence and power. That man may be distinguished
from the animal world and defined by his vices; that being
human is having the capacity to do evil wilfully—these features
millenarists find repugnant. And they assert themselves against
them. The implicit questions which they ask are: In what does
the dignity of man consist? How may the essential features of
integrity be revealed and measured? If current activities do not
reveal and measure selected qualities; and if the reward of
virtue is merely an unacknowledged self-esteem; then those
engaged in these transparently pointless endeavours will search
for guarantees of the worthwhileness of what they are doing not

only in their own eyes but also in the eyes of others. Because money may blur these essential measures, more often than not the 'economic issue' which gives momentum to a movement tends to hinge on the handling of money.

With the primary measures in doubt, individuals associate and put their different diagnoses and solutions to the test of external expression. But their activities will remain disorganized until a prophet appears. They may put flowers in vases, express themselves by drawing in the sand, comfort themselves with particularistic interpretations of myths and received traditions, or place their trust in private rituals and private opinions. But these activities are merely probings. Until a prophet emerges to symbolize the new man by concentrating these probings in himself and giving them coherence, the activities remain inchoate and disorganized. At the start, the personal qualities of a prophet seem to matter little. What is important is that his message should appear to come from a source beyond commonsense experience. It must be a revelation. Usually the message is claimed, or presumed, to have been revealed in a dream or vision or some other mystical experience. Whatever the cultural idiom, the message is taken to be beyond man's wit to devise. It is a divine revelation. It transcends the capacities of a man acting alone.

Some revelations appear nonsensical. Still, those who await a message remember them. Few prophets do not have precursors, and every revelation is of value as hope and expectation transmute what is, after all, not the product of one man's mind but the result of a power working through the medium of a particularly receptive person. A relevance—which must be socially significant—will appear in time. The revelation which pierces the impasse and carried men with it is usually one which echoes the theorizing and experimentation that has gone before. The particular economic issues are made explicit—('We must have buffalo, or land or manufactured goods; We should handle money thus and not so')—and instructions as to how particular activities will reveal integrity, the worthwhileness in being human, are given. Re-ordering economic activities to measure man effectively involves a political reorientation, and this in turn is grounded in those assumptions which guarantee the truth of things. So that, although much of what a prophet has to say is generally expressed in a mystical idiom, it also expresses and guarantees political objectives which will solve the economic issue. What is envisaged is a new condition of being, a new man. Often there are enactments of an initial non-human or pre-human state: a condition without rules and lacking in particular that fundamental rule of community life, the incest taboo. Thus an orgy of sexual promiscuity may be followed by a form of baptism and the entry into a new condition governed by fresh rules and assumptions. There may be dancing, shaking, quaking, trances, whirling and speaking with tongues as, plumbing more deeply into their experience, participants seek that inspiration which will guarantee their activities as right and founded in truth.

Phase 3

The third and last phase of the cycle is the aftermath. Sometimes, as organizational skills are deployed and the new assumptions begin to be firmly established, a sect develops. In other cases there follows a period of anti-climax and disillusion which then tends to redevelop into the first phase of intellectual probing, rumour-mongering and heightening emotional tensions. Failure to bring about the overt ends of the activities tends to restart the cycle: we recognize those outstanding figures we call precursor prophets. Partial successes are taken as evidence of having proceeded along the right lines. The drive is the imperative of finding a new redemptive process. To ask whether particular activities have 'succeeded' or 'failed' in attaining their overt objectives is, however, the wrong question. The issue is not a pole, or a flag, a load of canned meat or whether a ritual will make bullets actually turn into water, but a satisfactory measure of the nature of man. In this sense all millenarian activities succeed. They are 'experiments in measurement'. Only afterwards, with the wisdom of hindsight and in terms of actual consequences, may one judge just how far they have succeeded.

Let us now look at the general pattern in another way by turning again to Oceanic material. Apart from the Australian aborigines, who are wildbooters, all Oceanic peoples are traditionally horticulturalists who augment this basic subsistence activity of cultivating root crops by animal husbandry, fishing, foraging and hunting. Polynesians and Micronesians enjoyed relatively well developed and sophisticated hierarchical political institutions. Relative powers were based upon birth, command over others, and that access to lands and foreshore which either followed from the fact of birth or was allocated to those who chose to ally themselves to powerful men. Melanesians were primarily traders, egalitarian in outlook, who found prestige and influence through competitive productive capacity and trading turnover. Australians were organized into small gerontocracies in which prestige and influence depended upon intellectual attainments; that is, upon a knowledge of myths, rituals and ceremonials in relation to the exigencies of daily life. Valuables or treasure articles were found everywhere but were never common media of exchange. Nowhere among Oceanic peoples before the advent of the European was there money or anything like it. In all communities prestige and status depended on the demonstration of particular qualities in prescribed activities. Being virtually closed communities, in none of them could an individual opt out of customary restrictions and prescriptions and still be regarded as a member of community. Indeed, to opt out altogether was certain social death, and usually physical death as well.

For Melanesians, who measured one another in terms of productive capacity, turnover in trade, and the range, size, and number of exchange and feasting obligations, the most significant thing about Europeans was their extraordinary productive capacity. They seemed able to produce foodstuffs and artifacts of almost infinite range, variety and complexity in vast quantities. For Polynesians and Micronesians, on the other hand, the most important feature about white men was their power of command, their capacity to kill and exact obedience. Europeans had more *mana* than the most powerful and influential chief. Everywhere in Oceania, therefore—for the Australians either died in defence of their lands, or retreated into forests and desert where no white man chose to live—the native populations were faced with abilities which, in traditional terms, were better than their own best, and with which they could not hope to compete. The only real alternative to the Australian 'solution' of withdrawal and virtual isolation, of insulating the indigenous moral and prestige systems from the moneyed economy, was to enter the white man's world on terms acceptable to both parties. Yet as soon as we posit this alternative to withdrawal we demand precisely those utopian conditions which are the concern of millenarian movements. We are asking for a single social order in which the moral qualities of all men are measured against commonly accepted and acknowledged criteria. And since pieces of money are now being rubbed together in darker palms, we also have to ask how access to money may accurately reflect the moral qualities of man. Further, now that the formerly closed communities have been opened to the temptations of a wider and more complex economy and social order, we have to ask whether it is possible for the same money to have quite different types of value within the single socio-political order.

Not simply a common medium of exchange, money is a basic measure of man in a social order defined by complex and diverse forms of specialization. Money makes full-time and diversified specialization possible. In the indigenous prestige systems of Melanesia, only mature men could have any influence. But when money appeared the young had the readiest access to it through their labour, and they could outbid their seniors. On the other hand, when a young man settled down and married he re-entered the traditional prestige system and could no longer earn money. That is, unless Melanesians actually worked for Europeans in the European settled areas, they could not earn money. They could not make their work in the fields or at sea meaningful within the terms prescribed by Europeans. Either they could return to their villages and become men of stature in traditional terms without the aid of money, or they could remain in the European settled areas, with money, and be considered men of small account. Now suppose that Melanesian communities had some resource that Europeans wanted to buy with money, and that through this access to money they could participate more fully in the larger economic community. Suppose also that through money the indigenous prestige systems could fit neatly, as sub-systems, into the prestige system of the larger community. Suppose, too, that there was no colour bar, no feeling that black and white skins indicated mutually exclusive moral systems, and that opportunities for political involvement and responsibility were open to all. Suppose, in short, that Europeans and indigenous peoples were one moral community—would there have been millenarian movements in Melanesia?

Before answering this question, let us apply the same test to the Polynesian situation. Without the means of earning money, or using it within their own communities, Polynesians yet entered a world dependent on money. Through his command over money the worst kind of European or an otherwise contemptible Polynesian might command obedience from men of high rank in the native community. Moreover, since access to goods was not controlled by generally accepted and understood rules and values, the goods themselves must become prizes in a game with uncertain rules. Which is one reason why Maori and Pakeha had to distrust one another. Further, though the Maori were dependent on land and its exploitation for the operation of their own prestige system, access to money and European goods required that they sell and abandon their lands. And this contradiction was exacerbated by the fact that the heads of slain warriors also fetched money. So, because prestige also depended on fighting, the Maori sold heads and lands in order to buy muskets to take more heads which, sold for money, could buy more muskets. In turn, the muskets were used to wage war more effectively in order to gain prestige by taking over the lands of neighbours. Thus, if in this fever to gain land both Pakeha and Maori could be said to be playing the same game, each was doing so in terms of different sets of rules and conventions. And though both sides could invent new rules for themselves when it seemed convenient, only the Pakeha had that kind of power which could enforce an overt consent.

We may summarize as follows:

Phase 1

Disenfranchisement and severance; discussion and intellectual or quasi-intellectual endeavours.

Lone individuals seek the basis of a common experience.

Loss of integrity turning on:

(a) Qualitative measures:

Industriousness; capacities of intellect; courage or warfare.

   (b) Quantitative measure:
      Handling money.
   (At this point there may be a political accommodation.)

Phase 2
   Externalization of thoughts and ideas in activities.
   (a) Diffuse or inchoate activities, no prophet.
   (b) Economic issue; emergence of prophet; organized activities; transcendence of problems.

Phase 3
   Aftermath.
   Complete victory; or sect; or recurrence into Phase 1.

In reducing the events of a millenarian movement to a pattern we have inevitably provided some kind of explanation of them. Here, bearing in mind the relations it has with religion and the redemptive process, the events of millenarian movements have been strung together on the theme of integrity. And we have also done something else. For in attempting to set out the conditions under which millenarian activities might seem unnecessary, we have almost begun to ignore inescapable facts about the nature of power and prestige. We have started to envisage a single moral order. We ourselves, that is, are beginning to envisage a kind of millennium, are beginning to participate in the first phase of a millenarian movement.

10

Explanation (i)[1]

In reviewing the problems of an internal classification of millenarian activities we saw how a variety of labels might lead an investigator into appreciating the kind of movement he was dealing with. But these labels were hardly adequate for discriminating between sets of relations. Such a classification can only be grounded in a prior conceptual framework. In looking for a general pattern we saw how the most positive component, the economic issue, could not be appreciated in isolation from the prestige system which, in its turn, could be related to four primary measures of man. Finally, in suggesting conditions in which a millenarian movement might seem unnecessary, we detected ourselves behaving as if we were in the first phase of a millenarian movement. In short, since the central issue is the enoblement of the nature of man, there are no known conditions which would render millenarian activities unnecessary.

This raises an important point. Is there much sense in attempting to account for a millenarian movement in the terms of an explanation which does not recognize as significant important features of these activities?

Consider the divine revelation experienced by the prophet. An anthropological 'explanation' is grounded in a synthesis between the participants' terms of reference and what one likes to think of as more objective criteria. Given the action, two kinds of rationalization meet in 'explanation'. But if we are confronted with the evidence of a divine revelation, we cannot declare it irrelevant or irrational or fantasy or wishful thinking. We must take it seriously and try to account for what actually occurs. Even if our own private assumptions do not admit of

[1] The most useful leading references are, perhaps, *Cohn*; *Emmett*; *Fuchs*; *Inglis*; *Jarvie* (3); *Lanternari*; *Linton*; *Stanner*; *Wallace*; *Worsley*.

such a thing as a divine revelation, we must admit that for
others it does exist. Nor, in meeting this requirement, is there any
call to be needlessly mystical about it. Whether revealed by
God, Jehovah, or the devil, this or that spirit, godling or deity,
or in a dream or vision; whether we describe it as an intuitive
grasp, or as the result of some psychological or physiological
process; however we try to describe or explain it we have to
confess that we know only a little about what happens. How
or why is an appropriate message received? How or why does it
become transmissible and seen to be appropriate by others? We
know that it occurs in every human group. We know that,
because of it, activities may cohere into an organized movement. We must take it into account, bending our own assumptions to meet it. But in doing so we should remember that we
are dealing with the creative act itself, with an emergent
rationality, with a process that discovers new rules and assumptions, new ways of distinguishing and classifying what is relevant, new ways of ignoring what seems irrelevant.

Within these terms, then, we may consider four general
types of explanation: the 'Psycho-physiological', the 'Ethnographic', the 'Marxist' and the 'Hegelian'. Convenient labels,
the four terms merely indicate packages of kinds of explanation
that seem, internally, to be closely related to each other. The
first is outside our present terms of reference but something
must be said because it may be in this field that the most
satisfactory 'total explanations' will eventually be given. With
the remaining three we are more closely concerned. All are
historical explanations. Insofar as they can be generalized they
become sociological explanations. Yet few writers take a standpoint that is exclusively contained in any one of the packages.
Most are eclectics, fishing in a variety of psychologies and
sociologies and ultimately imposing on the data their own
millenarian intuitions. The result is an embarrassing wealth of
explanatory models, some clearly repetitive, and others whose
subtleties and ambiguities of language often make it difficult to
see in what respects they are distinct. We propose now a general
review of how far these kinds of explanation can take us.

THE PSYCHO-PHYSIOLOGICAL

Stemming largely from Pavlov's work on dogs and some of the more practical consequences of his results, like 'brain washing' or 'thought control', much has been done to explain the mechanics of religious conversion.[1] We think we know, roughly, what kinds of conditions impinging on the human brain are likely to result in that re-orientation which we commonly describe as 'conversion'—a quite new appreciation of the significance of the relations between the self and the outside world. Granted, however, that neuro-physiology can tell us precisely what has happened and is going on in the *brains* of those who participate in millenarian activities, it can tell us little about the *minds* of the participants or what their thoughts are. Nor does neuro-physiology pretend to explain why these brain processes should be set in train at a particular time in a particular place. Further, given the same conditions of shock and disorientation followed by the presentation of a defined new orientation, neuro-physiology cannot tell us why on some occasions the changes in the brain that might be expected to occur do not occur. The only recourse is to built-in proclivities or resistances. In short, though neuro-physiology can tell us what happens to the brain, and can, by creating prescribed conditions in the laboratory or clinic, actually set these brain processes in train, in the end explanation is grounded in the social context. Why should resistances or proclivities be built-in? Quite apart, therefore, from our own terms of reference which force us to seek explanations of a sociological kind, we have the perhaps dubious comfort of knowing that if a 'total explanation' is available it will be grounded in that social context from which the impulse to neuro-physiological research springs. On the other hand, a reverse train of thought—referring social conditions to psycho-physiological conditions—occurs with great frequency.

First, a simple example. After having described with exemplary precision the history of a Melanesian millenarian movement, and after having accurately summarized the main features of the movement—without however bringing these features into significant relations with each other—an author

[1] See *Sargant.*

concludes that movements of this kind 'provide refuge and
consolation as an unpractical solution to ever-increasing
difficulties.'[1] Now whether this statement was meant as a conclusion, or as a reflection, it constitutes in itself a reduction to
the terms of the commonsense psychology of a particular culture. Given that in our own folk experience people who are
desperately in need of refuge and consolation are apt to do odd
things, those who do odd things are clearly looking for refuge
and consolation. The statement is self-evident, sums up what
seems to be the gist of the matter; the people concerned really
do seem to have been in need of refuge and consolation. But is
this the kind of conclusion that an anthropologist should like
to reach? It is also true, if it is not wholly a truism, that Melanesian cargo cults could be regarded as a 'symbolic way of dealing with problems which cannot be cannot be dealt with in any
other way.'[2] What is being usefully said here? Writing of the
same movements, Firth makes much the same point much more
explicitly: 'Blocked on the one side by inadequate resources,
lack of training, and lack of opportunity from creating the
desired goods for themselves, and on the other side by lack of
knowledge from realizing the necessary technical and economic
steps required before the goods can come to their shores, the
New Guinea natives have turned to fantasy. They seek their
satisfaction in an imaginative projection.'[3] Again, this is true up
to a point, and it goes beyond mere commonsense. But one may
still ask whether other kinds of conclusion that are specifically
anthropological or sociological are not possible.

More holistic psychological explanations which are at least
grounded in a systematic universe of discourse rather than in
folk psychology, are contained in ideas that root millenarian
activities in 'The World's Great Anxiety-Dream',[4] or in
'Anxiety-Separation',[5] or in 'Deprivation',[6] or, more widely and
explicitly, in the 'Psychology of the Participants'.[7] 'If one
would arrive at an adequate interpretation . . .' writes Cohn of
medieval millenarian movements, 'one cannot afford to ignore
the psychic content of the phantasies which have inspired them.
All these phantasies are precisely such as are commonly found

[1] *Allan*, p. 84.   [2] *Beattie*, p. 70.   [3] *Firth*, p. 113.
[4] *Fulop-Miller*, pp. 3–17.
[5] *de Grazia* (i) ff.   [6] *Thrupp*, p. 26.   [7] *Kaminsky*, p. 216.

in individual cases of paranoia. The megalomaniac view of one-self as the elect, wholly good, abominably persecuted yet assured of ultimate triumph; the attribution of gigantic and demonic powers to the adversary; the refusal to accept the ineluctable limitations and imperfections of human existence, such as transience, dissension, conflict, fallibility whether in-tellectual or moral; the obsession with inerrable prophecies—these attitudes are symptoms which together constitute the unmistakable syndrome of paranoia. But a paranoiac delusion does not cease to be so because it is shared by so many indi-viduals, nor yet because those individuals have real and ample grounds for regarding themselves as victims of oppression'.[1] On the other hand, granted that paranoia often runs schizophrenia pretty close, Sargant comes down heavily on a basic schizo-phrenic condition.[2]

These kinds of explanation or interpretation are no doubt 'true' or 'sufficient for the purpose'. But while it is perhaps inevitable that many of European background and culture should seek their 'final' explanations in fields which seem to be more positively grounded, more scientific and certain than sociology presently is, the fact that these universes of know-ledge take departure from sets of assumptions that are social in nature should encourage, rather than deter us from searching, for a sociological explanation. There is little doubt that many a millenarian movement could accurately be described as a 'psychological reaction to cultural inadequacy',[3] or as—because the participants often do suffer—a 'propensity to suffer',[4] or, because a movement has in fact occurred, as an innate or 'cul-tural disposition'[5] on the parts of the participants to participate. Yet if statements such as these are not merely variations of the proposition 'it is, therefore it is or must be', or simply shorthand characterizations, it is not easy to see in what ways they carry a meaning that is not obvious at the outset. Allowing that 'aesthetic attraction',[6] 'dramatic projection',[7] or 'symbolic means',[8] may have significant sociological content, the moment we ask why they should have any importance at all we are back to 'anxiety', 'consolation' and the rest: a short-circuit back to

[1] *Cohn*, p. 309.   [2] *Sargant*, p. 51.   [3] *Bruijn*, pp. 9–10.
[4] *Thrupp*, p. 26.   [5] *Thrupp*; *Inglis*.   [6] *Thrupp*, p. 26.
[7] *Firth* (5), p. 113.   [8] *Beattie*, p. 70.

those words whose behavioural content among ourselves we never tire of trying to elucidate.

It may be of course that these kinds of explanation are not only 'proper in the circumstances' but, because they return us to our own cultural assumptions, are as it were 'final explanations'. For, other than having recourse to 'divine providence'—which is at least an explanation referred to something conceived of as outside ourselves and our cultural inheritance—those of European culture are wont to proceed on, and return to, biologically or psychologically derived assumptions. Even if anthropologists or sociologists become adequate to their subjects, and succeed in finding kinds of explanation that transcend the limits of a particular cultural experience, it is difficult to see how their explanations will totally escape becoming regrounded in human biology—which presumes to transcend cultural limitations—and their own culturally derived notions of the nature of the human psyche. We understand and like these kinds of explanation. They are a useful shorthand, they come quite 'naturally' to us, and, as has been said of cargo cults, 'they serve to explain the inexplicable'.[1] Nevertheless, these kinds of ethnocentricism hardly become an anthropologist. His task is to widen the prospects of knowledge of man's condition, not reduce them. Those who seek a new integrity are not necessarily psychologically disorientated, subject to fantasy or unable to explain themselves.

THE 'ETHNOGRAPHIC'

An 'ethnographic explanation' attempts to show why, in particular places and at particular times, millenarian activities have occurred. Such an explanation is historical in the sense that it does not explain why, in other places or at different times, under the same general conditions, millenarian activities did not take place. And an explanation which cannot account for the negative as well as the positive instance can only be a temporary explanation. If we allow that a diffuse form of phase 2—flowers in vases, diagrams in the sand—may represent a continuum, then, if only for purposes of argument, the problem is narrowed to explaining why a movement should gain a positive coherence through the emergence of a prophet.

[1] *Belshaw* (1).

But it is precisely in this respect that good anthropological
evidence is lacking. Trained investigators are rarely on the spot
and second-hand evidence must suffice. While it is true that
such historical evidence as we have of European millenarian
movements has been investigated by neuro-physiologists,[1] and
we may learn much from them as to how activities cohere into a
movement, the why of it remains mysterious.

So far as an 'ethnographic' explanation is a general statement
about relations of power, so far do we have a crude sociological
explanation. Thus, for example, in the typical European colonial
situation relations between white men and black men, most
evident in the relations between the administration and the
native community, can become relations between rulers and
ruled. We could expand on this by noting that authority was
virtually absolute; that the rulers monopolized economic
resources and the means of controlling and exploiting the common environment; that the subordinate community had little
say in the matter, could not check the rulers, and in any case
understood little about the techniques used by the rulers.
Further, noting that the political regime was permissive, we
might look for a missionary or someone who, whether or not in
clerical garb and irrespective of the colour of his skin, was
communicating to the subordinate community some understanding of the assumptions which guided the actions of those
in authority—thus stirring doubts and uncertainties and also
indicating ways in which authority might be outflanked and
the stranglehold broken.

Most 'ethnographic' accounts move towards this kind of
formulation even if, inevitably, they become trapped in particular categories at the expense of the more general. If 'race
relations', for example, blind one to relations of hierarchy, the
empirical evidence is nonetheless adduced, observations are
provided with a context, and explanation is offered in terms of
relative significances in the light of the context. Clearly, therefore, the context, and predispositions towards a particular context, become the most important elements.

The most unsatisfactory kinds of context are those which are
based on a primary distinction between the rational and
irrational, or between reality and fantasy. Invariably the

[1] *Sargant.*

investigator thinks of himself as rational, and the participants in a millenarian movement as irrational or given to fantasy. Yet this sort of explanation has one great advantage: since all men may sometimes be given to fantasy, and may act 'irrationally', it satisfactorily explains both positive and negative instances. The drawback is that such a method of explanation cannot be heuristic. It can yield no new knowledge. Secure in his own unquestioned premises and assumptions the investigator may describe, analyse and pass judgement in a single breath. In principle such an explanation scarcely differs from that of the lady who, in a letter to the author, was perfectly satisfied with her judgement on cargo movements that 'They only want something for nothing'. Indeed, because it is simple and begs no questions, because it proceeds directly from our own assumptions regarding social life, many would prefer the last as an adequate summing-up of the problem. The fact remains, however, that outside the context of a millenarian movement almost all types of social behaviour have been shown to yield to the assumption 'rational in the circumstances, given the premises'. Few scholars would today consider an explanation that involved the oppositions rational/irrational or reality/fantasy as determinitive when examining activities that were not millenarian movements. Why then use them in relation to millenarian movements? On the other hand the kind of explanation that proceeds from the assumption of 'wishful thinking' may be forgiven. For in this case it becomes possible to explore the implications of 'wishful thinking', and in doing so to unravel the premises on which a millenarian movement appears to be based—thus providing a framework of sets of relations within terms of which another movement might be examined. Gradually such a framework could be qualified and altered so as to include in its ambit further varieties of expression.

Between these two extremes we may isolate four general types of 'ethnographic' explanation. The first, exemplified by Bryan Wilson, in his *Sects and Society*, accepts 'the hypothesis that religious movements, as essentially social movements, can be expected to stand in specific relations to social classes, to their prevailing economic and social conditions, and to the cultural and social ethos obtaining within such groups'.[1] Three

[1] *Wilson*, p. 14.

religious groups are investigated and, though there may be disagreements as to what the nature of 'specific relations' should be, conclusions are reached in terms of the features of these relations. Thus, 'The ideal-type established sect in Christianity is an essentially minority religious movement, stressing doctrines, practices or experience which are divergent from those of the orthodox religious groups. It is divergent from, and may be in opposition to, all other teachings: it regards its own body of doctrine and practice as the truth which it possesses, in full measure, to the exclusion of all other groups. Usually it considers its message to be a distinct restoration, or retention, of primitive apostolic Christianity, and it relies directly on the Word of God, or special commentary on that Word, supposed alone to interpret it aright: it may accept inspiration from God additional to the Bible. Membership is essentially voluntary; merit is a prerequisite to admission, and demerit in these terms a subject of discipline and perhaps dismissal. A special relation is posited between the believer and Jesus Christ, and association with him in a particular way may constitute a membership requirement. The sect gathers a select group aside and—dissociating itself from the traditions of the institutional church—it seeks to validate its position by reference to superhuman authority, of a traditional or charismatic kind, or of both. The sect is without historical sense, and its self-interpretation describes its own mission as uniquely the purpose of God, and its own emergence as of special significance in the schemes of God. It is without a paid ministry and its leaders are unprofessional, arising from the lay following of the movement; they may be regarded as supernaturally endowed although this is more usual of the founder of the movement. It regards itself as apart from the secular society, and considers itself to have a superior ethic, resting on its distinctive ideology. Its members are counselled to keep separate from the world. The sect is typically totalitarian, seeking to organize, or to dominate the way of life of adherents, often making a particular way of life a condition of blessing here or hereafter. There tends to be a distinctive social pattern, the rejection of folk-ways of the wider society, and the acceptance of particular practices held as essential to the good way of life.'[1]

[1] *Wilson*, p. 326.

In this type of study, while the structure of the 'ethos' from which the movement takes departure is left a little vague, to be apprehended from the movement itself, or taken for granted, the 'prevailing economic and social conditions' are adduced in great detail. And in this respect it is in contrast with our second type of 'ethnographic' explanation which, though it may analyse or describe the social and economic conditions in great detail, rests its case not on a perhaps vague 'ethos', but on a firmly structured intellectual or philosophical tradition. And if this tradition may also be theological it is nonetheless intellectual and philosophical whether or not it is more, or less, precisely defined. Thus, for example, in his study of the Fifth Monarchy Men, Rogers rests his case on the detail of the inspirational source (The Book of Daniel, Chapter VII, v. 1–27; Revelations, Chapter XIII, v. 1–7) on the one hand, and a much more vaguely defined ethos on the other. 'Millenarian enthusiasm had always flourished', he writes, 'when men thought and cared deeply about religion, and when political convulsions tempted them to deduce that the time of the end was approaching. . . . Fifth Monarchism was essentially a creed of the seventeenth century. In the eighteenth century, an age of reason and growing scepticism, and of internal stability, the ethos was lacking, and millenarianism declined into insignificance. . . .'[1] Though Rogers' history is at fault, he goes on to say that '. . . the views of the Fifth Monarchy men were a harking-back to the medieval conception that religion should embrace and control every aspect of human life. In the sense that this conception was contrary to the tendency towards the secularization of political thought which had set in since the reformation, the ideas of the Fifth Monarchy men were not only unrealistic, but an anachronism also.'[2]

Of much vaster proportions in every way than Rogers' study, but adopting in principle much the same approach, Monsignor Knox's authoritative[3] investigation into the millenarian or Enthusiastic movements that *did* take place in the eighteenth century is not only precise about historical connections and sources, but is also firm and detailed about the intellectual and philosophical tradition from which the movements concerned took departure. What is mainly missing, or naïvely treated when

---

[1] *Rogers*, p. 132.   [2] *Rogers*, p. 155.   [3] *Knox*.

approached, are the 'specific relations' of these movements to extant 'social classes' and the 'prevailing economic and social conditions'. Aside from the historical narrative, the context provided by Knox consists of three parts. First, there are the features which spell out the nature of Enthusiasm: the revolt against the established discipline, harking back to a supposed golden age of early Christianity; direct inspiration leading to antinomianism;[1] rigorism;[2] ecstasies; shakings; fits; trances and the like; a looking forward to the millennium. Second, these familiar features are linked through an historico-intellectual tradition to the troubles which Paul had with the Corinthians, troubles which drew from Paul some of his finest letters, troubles which, on the evidence of the letters, seem to have been typically millenarian; bigotry, prophesyings, detachment from established assumptions. Thirdly, the movements are rooted in an opposition between an augustinian platonism on the one hand and a more formal and rigid aristotelianism on the other.[3] Thus, the Divine Fact being given, reason is divorced from religion, and religion becomes something to do with the senses or emotions. Prayer being an interior activity, there is a direct link between the soul and God: hence rites, liturgy, sacraments and the priesthood—the organizational framework of a religious congregation—are deemed unnecessary. This direct, personal and individual approach to the Divine Presence involves a new theology of Grace, quite opposed to the established and traditional view that Grace is mediated through, and secreted in, the institutions of an organized sacramental life. Just as there may be no barriers to accesses of Grace—and almost every traditional religious activity such as music, the use of images, pictures, intellect and reason is considered a barrier—so enthusiasts cannot abide to be 'almost Christians'. Yet such

---

[1] Shorter *O.E.D.*: 'One who maintains that the moral law is not binding upon Christians, under the law of grace 1645.'

In a broader sense the word refers to a state of positive lawlessness in which persons may seek their own exclusive rules.

[2] A strict adherence to explicit rules.

[3] Briefly, this means an opposition between on the one hand assumptions which ascribe 'reality' to the images and thoughts of the mind, whether these appear as gods, demons, witches, words or ideals, and on the other hand assumptions which ascribe 'reality' primarily only to that which is rooted in matter.

severities must result in scandal and lapses. Hence the alternations of rigorism and antinomianism. Ultimately, however, if the movement is to survive it must become organized and institutionalized. Nevertheless, even when institutionalized, the sect still reflects the basic oppositions with which it started, and so germinates the seeds of further splitting from the newly established socio-religious body. Millenarists cannot abide the corruption that organization necessarily entails.

In referring the historical events which he is considering not so much to the objective symbolic system but to his own and his subjects' views of the symbolic system, Knox is adopting much the same approach as that of many anthropologists.[1] But there is this difference. Whereas Knox's view is derived from a heritage of symbols and thoughts about them which he shares with his readers, an anthropologist has first to render intelligible a symbolic system and mode of understanding which his readers do not share. And the strangeness of a particular cultural idiom, combined with the linguistic difficulties of an anthropologist attempting to translate and communicate that which can be only approximately translated, often tend to obscure what seem to be similar behavioural processes. An explanation which takes departure from a series of 'transactions'[2] with the gods is surely but one expression of that reality of which specific theories of Grace and redemption are others.

Our third type of 'ethnographic' explanation lumps together those many authors who, themselves highly critical of colonial administrative practices, have sought to emphasize those features of millenarian movements which reveal economic and political problems. Given that such problems derive as often as not from the utopian views of particular authors, we find in their works, nevertheless, a sharpening of political and economic contexts. Millenarian movements are regarded as expressive of economic difficulties and political discontents. Analysis is directed towards the probable causes of these ills in the total body social, and particular measures are suggested which might alleviate them. The reader is provided with impressively detailed descriptions and analyses of the economic and political conditions in which the movements had their genesis. Such

[1] Particularly *Stanner*.   [2] *Stanner.*

explanations are essentially philanthropic, though believed to be practical, and are addressed, implicitly if not explicitly, to similarly motivated colleagues and against the political regime in control. Rooted in a long and well-established tradition of English political and economic life, these kinds of approach account for the main bulk of the literature on millenarian movements in English. The basic premise, explicitly or implicitly, is that millenarian movements are symptomatic of faulty administration, inequitable accesses to resources, and a defective distribution of political rights and obligations. Consequently, to take up the medical (or biological) metaphor again, explanation takes the form of diagnosing particular maladies and recommending, again either explicitly or implicitly, a variety of cures.[1]

In such kinds of explanation the definitive feature of a millenarian movement will not receive much attention. It seems irrelevant to the discussion. Since nothing very much can be done about a divine revelation in any case, the main effort is directed towards those aspects of the problem which will yield to positive analysis and subsequent action. Hence it is that so many millenarian movements and activities can be dismissed as 'irrational'. Given that millenarian activities spring from imperfect conditions, and that the improvement of these conditions lies in the notion of the perfectability of economic and political conditions, it is irrational to seek improvement by what seems to be a neglect of just those features which can be perfected. Pragmatic, ever seeking after details of authentic evidence, such studies have immeasurably increased our knowledge of the conditions in which millenarian movements occur. They do not explain why, in similar conditions, millenarian movements do not occur, nor do they pretend to do so. For where millenarian movements do not occur, no problem is evident. On the other hand political and economic problems are always waiting to be solved. Thus it is only by accident that these kinds of explanation tell us anything about millenarian movements *per se*. At the same time, all such studies are, or attempt to be, sociological. They tell us of sets of relations within which millenarian movements occurred.

A fourth kind of 'ethnographic' explanation is represented by purely historical descriptions and narratives. Here the reader is

[1] For example, *Belshaw* (1) and (2); *Guiart* (1) and (2).

left to draw many of his own conclusions. Abstract formulations
of relations are rarely explicit, often ambiguous. Features of
relatedness tend to derive from the author's personal predispositions, and the reader is invited to impose his own interpretation on the events described and on such qualities of
relationship as may be adduced. Time rather than logic is the
connecting principle. That which is prior in time is thought of as
'cause', and that which comes after is 'effect'. There is little
awareness of logic as timeless, or of that vision of the future
which has so much to do with making the present. Yet the
fullest and most complete accounts of millenarian movements
are generally of this kind.[1] It may be that the wealth of detail
defies sociological explanation. Perhaps an historian's pre-
occupation with the concrete events prevents an appreciation
of the logic of social relations. But in most cases, one feels, it is
because the author wanted it to be that way: a report, a narrative of what happened.

Such accounts explain by implication. They often include
masses of detail which may or may not turn out to be sociologically relevant: the circumstances and life history of the
prophet; significant experiences in the lives of those participating; accounts and explanations of both participants and outside observers. The particular and contingent tends to be
explained at the expense of the more general and persistent,
the narrative theme carries a personal and ethnocentricized
logic of its own.

THE 'MARXIST'

Even where they satisfy the sociological requirements of being
related to more abstract categories or sets or relations, 'ethnographic' explanations still tend to be particularistic. Mainly this
is because of the lack of a commonly accepted 'sociological
language', and the diversity of particular sociologies. Thus
though most would agree that sociology is concerned with
relations on the level of the collective, it is open to dispute
whether these relations should be 'real' or 'logical', whether or
not and in what circumstances these two categories do or should
correspond with each other, whether the features to be related

[1] See *Williams, F. E.* (1) and (2); *Lawrence* (2).

should be in terms of the categories of the investigator or investigated, and whether the fundamental units are categories or groups or activities or institutions. Nor, since all sociology must spring from moral conviction based on particular kinds of assumptions, and western European culture is characterized by diversities of moral conviction, is the lack of a general consensus at all surprising. On the other hand, within this characteristically eclectic ambience there is one kind of sociology that is positive, well known both as myth and in its substance, and which commands a wider acceptance than other kinds of sociology: the 'Marxist'.

For the early Christian, steeped in his pentecostal tradition, millenarian activities would require little external explanation. Directly apprehended within terms of the Christian experience, millenarian movements would simply pose the problem of deciding on their truth or falsity, whether they were derived from the right or wrong source, whether they were inspired by the Holy Spirit or the devil. Early Christians, Saint Paul especially, were most concerned with determining the criteria on which to make this kind of judgement. Accepting the fact of divine revelation, and the recurrence of divine inspiration, the early Church sought to contain the more bizarre consequences of this acceptance within highly organized, but diversified, institutional forms. It developed an elaborate apparatus for deciding questions of schism, heresy, true or false inspirations, possession by the Spirit or by the devil and his minions. The 'Marxist' explanation takes this tradition forward. Being itself millenarian, Marxism can, like the early Christian, explain a millenarian movement in terms of its own postulates and experience. On the other hand, denying the deity or divine interventions, the 'Marxist' cannot explain the prophet and his inspiration. Positive and materialist, it prefers to regard the prophet as irrelevant, accidental, or at most as occupying a socially determined role, an ambiguous and unnecessary catalyst in a developmental process that might be more rationally achieved and ordered without him. Concentrating on features of conflict in social relations, Marxism seeks to explain the conflict between groups or classes of persons by referring to a continuing process of competition for resources: the materialist historical dialectic. And though some may dispute the extent to which Marxism is, or should be, concerned with social groups rather than with logical categories and relations, on the whole and in practice the tendency must be towards the more positive; towards identifying the conflict as existing between groups or classes of people.

Millenarian movements clearly indicate situations of conflict which are part of a continuing historical process. Nor are these conflicts, or their sources, necessarily resolved by a political regime which puts an end to the movement itself. Considered to derive from internal contradictions within the total body social, such occurrences may be neatly dovetailed into the 'Marxist' experience. In English hands, moreover, 'Marxist' explanations cannot but be coloured by that much longer tradition of philanthropic valetudinarianism which, itself the child of more orthodox and specifically religious millenarianism, is a part of all English radical thought. Thus two birds may be killed with one stone. The while the maladies (conflicts) affecting the body social are being diagnosed, identified and related to one another, a sociological explanation is offered which goes further than a series of recommendations to the administrative authority or political regime. Seizing on the politico-economic features of the situation, the movement may be broken down into a number of inequities (conflicts) concerned with competing powers over the disposal of economic resources. In the colonial situation the white-black, European-native, administration-administrated, money-users and non-money-users relationships provide a ready-made class conflict. The way in which the capitalist system, or a free-market economy,[1] enriches the rich and impoverishes the poor is clear-cut and needs little demonstration. If there are difficulties with the facts of pre-industrial economies without money, or where money is used not as money but as treasure articles, one may either regard the colonial situation as an extension of the metropolitan environment, or find a revolutionary situation between those who make capital and cash and those who cannot but lose them.

Unrivalled in its ability to lay bare the positive components of social relations in terms of the deployment of various kinds of wealth and property, and so revealing the constitutive elements

[1] Or a free-market economy in contact with a subsistence economy.

of present or future conflict, a 'Marxist' explanation forces us to see the concrete problems of real people. We also begin to appreciate the conflict in relative terms. No matter how much more wealthy in an absolute sense an indigenous community may be as the result of European penetration, so long as the gap between European and native commands over resources continues to widen, so long is the conflict exacerbated rather than assuaged. By all means set up local councils or soviets which allow indigenous communities a share in managing their own affairs. But if by so doing the power of the central authority is increased, further conflict is implied. And the same kinds of relations seem to exist where, within a moneyed environment, lone individuals see themselves inevitably becoming poorer in relation to those in privileged or established positions, who seem to be becoming even more prosperous. Here lies the dilemma. For the politico-economic conflict evident in millenarian movements is also a conflict between two quite different kinds of prestige system on the one hand, and two different kinds of understanding on the other.

Mutual understanding is clearly a pre-condition for creating a single moral order or resolving a conflict. But understanding of itself cannot bring about the reconciliation of different prestige systems. In the colonial situation the kinds of prestige implied by 'subsistence community' on the one hand and 'complex community' on the other, are mutually opposed. And in the variety of attitudes towards money one may see an overriding impulse to learn how to use money effectively. Similarly, within the traditionally moneyed environment attempts to assert a right to handle money differently are impressive. In both situations the question hinges on the discovery of satisfactory qualitative measures within a social ambience determined by a quantitative system.

How resolve the dilemma? A capitalist democracy, inhibited from resorting to outright physical coercion, by definition permissive, and in any case unwilling to undertake action because of the expense involved, may wrestle with its conscience, compromise, or put its faith in time the great healer or some sort of evolutionary process. But the Marxist who is backed by the powers of a Marxist government need have no such hesitations. For, being in itself a relatively young millenarian movement,

Marxism, in order to resolve these otherwise highly intractable problems, may have recourse to the same kinds of certain, absolute and highly persuasive sanctions as are used in the movements we have instanced. However sceptical of a prophet and his revelation they may be, the lone individuals who are coming into association, or who have just come into association, are virtually forced to participate in a movement by a variety of stringent sanctions. On the one hand there are the posited advantages of remaining in association, on the other the alternative of again becoming a lone individual. The rigorism of millenarian movements within the European tradition is matched by the rigorism of such activities within the colonial situation. In the former case condemnation to hell fire and the disgrace of expulsion accompany the loneliness of severance; in the latter case those who do not participate in the rites will be swallowed in a holocaust, will forfeit cargo, will not become invulnerable to European bullets. These are hard and persuasive threats, difficult to resist even if one were not caught up in the excitement and hysteria which many millenarian movements involve. But the practising Marxist with power, burdened with the responsibility of actually realizing the millennium in materialist terms, may enforce participation in the movement by sanctions which are nonetheless daunting for not being cast in a mystical idiom. As with many other millenarian movements, and as with those who are millennially inclined, Marxism lays claim to truths that are trans-culturally valid.

At this point the Marxist explanation ceases to explain something exterior to itself. It begins to explain itself in terms of its own assumptions. It uses another millenarian movement to explain itself to itself. At the same time, since it contains within itself a practical programme for action, Marxism does face fairly and squarely the real and concrete problem of creating *de novo* and relatively quickly a single prestige system with commonly held rules and conventions backed by assumptions which guarantee and enforce their truth and validity. But whether a man succeeds in exerting his influence over millions, a few dozen who will form the nucleus of a smaller community within the greater, or seems to fail entirely, this is precisely what the prophet in a millenarian movement is attempting to do in a mystical idiom without the aid of material powers. Participating in an action programme, whether as settler, underprivileged weaver, administrator-missionary bearing the white man's burden, welfare officer, revolutionary, or farmer or drover, no millenarist can doubt the overall validity of the truths he believes he has grasped. Dire sanctions and physical coercion seem necessary to the creation of a single moral order. Moderation tends to result in the creation of numerous and separate but more or less mutually consistent moral orders within a greater whole.

It is surely the characteristic permissiveness of the Christian tradition and experience which allows varieties of millennia to be envisaged, seems to encourage the occurrence of millenarian activities, and often inhibits the political regime from moving against them with the firmness and decision necessary to extirpate them. Nevertheless, on many occasions Christians themselves have been the reverse of permissive. Their separate moral orders, related to particularist interests, may develop so as to create their own discords between one another. And when that occurs it provides us with the context of co-existing and competing moral orders within which we can perceive the meaning of the millennium: peace, a cutting of the Gordian knot of doubt, uncertainty and conflict in order to find freedom from dilemma, cares and responsibility. Although in practice a condition of being in which all desires are satisfied and therefore expunged is rarely realized, every millenarist believes he has grasped the secret and is driven to enforce it on others. Millenarian movements breed themselves.

Marxism holds much the same promise as other millenarian movements, and it is as keen to enforce its particular millennium. Yet as many a disappointed prophet has found, corruption and the human are synonymous. Given the prospect of peace and release from desire, people wander back to their crops and their cares. Provided with an opportunity for egalitarian bliss, some prefer to be better than others, want to control others, prefer to become aware of their worth by competing and dealing with others. These features a prophet must reconcile with peace and no conflict; these features Marxism seeks to contain.

'Ethnographic' explanations tend to be eclectic, including large chunks of the personal and intuitive. They are forever trapped in a hierarchy of rationalizations upon the action. The 'Marxist' explanation, on the other hand, resolves this dilemma by referring all rationalizations to the positive and objective feature of economic advantage. And there are of course many variations of the 'Marxist' explanation.[1] Sometimes mixed in with Freudian psychology, sometimes projected back into a psychology of 'deprivation',[2] and a part of every 'ethnographic' or socio-historical explanation, Marxism takes the Christian tradition from the bonfire of the French revolution and the Age of Reason and replants it in the material instead of the divine. Like the early Christian, and with a Christian's peculiar regard for history and time—but denying the validity of that mystical experience with which all millenarian movements commence, and substituting the criterion of material advantage—a Marxist can explain the millennial features of a politico-economic movement in terms of true or false, opportune or inopportune, well founded or misguided. And it has developed an apparatus by which it can decide such questions. What a 'Marxist' explanation cannot do, because its assumptions exclude it from the relevant, is explain the divine intervention demonstrated by the prophet.

THE 'HEGELIAN'

Unlike a 'Marxist' explanation, the 'Hegelian' attempts to make use of a total experience both to explain itself as well as to explain other kinds of social order, experience or tradition. Specifically including the mystical experience, an 'Hegelian' explanation attempts to explain a smaller whole in the terms of a larger, a relatively narrow experience in the terms of a relatively wider. It assumes, but is not specific about, a wider body of knowledge than is possessed by investigator and investigated. For us this means that explanation must be in terms of categories which comprehend the rationalizations of both the anthropologist and the people he is studying. Further, it assumes a generalized purpose in human affairs. While the 'Marxist' explanation uses its materialist experience to explain the more positive components of a millenarian movement, an

---

[1] See, for example, *Worsley*; *Mukerjee*; *Lanternari*.
[2] *Thrupp*.

'Hegelian' explanation, framed within the terms of an abstract historical dialectic, admits the operations of a transcendent power. This a 'Marxist' explanation cannot allow. It does not matter whether we identify this power as 'divine', 'charismatic', the 'Will of God', the 'Spirit of History', the 'Evolutionary Process', 'Instinct' or anything else. It is enough that we have some reference for the empirically verifiable and definitive feature of a millenarian movement: the revelation. We cannot disregard it. By giving the revelation a reference, however vague, we can move from what we know something about to what we know little about. We may gain some insight into the prophet and his persuasiveness. On the other hand, we should be on our guard against a terminology which in pretending to explain only explains away. What is important is that, whether brought about by some short circuit in the brain process,[1] or by some happy fusion or juxtaposition of categories hitherto regarded as distinct,[2] a revelation occurs: it is creative and represents a new synthesis.

In recognizing the existence of a force whose nature we do not yet understand, an 'Hegelian' explanation is clearly exploratory, and therefore potentially fruitful. The attempt to explain enlarges our own cultural experience and, instead of explaining Oceanic, American, Asian or African millenarian movements in terms of ourselves, we explain both ourselves and the culturally dissimilar millenarian movement in terms of something that has become larger than either. By recognizing what he chose to name 'charisma', Weber[3] was enabled not only to unravel features of political and economic conflict, but also to some extent to penetrate the meaning of charisma. Now charisma and charismatic have become part of the vocabulary of every-day discourse. And a prophet has charismatic qualities. To go further and assume that a prophet is moved by an impersonal historical force is, perhaps, unnecessarily mystical. Nevertheless, if only as a heuristic device, the idea or assumption that there might indeed be a definable impersonal historical force puts us into a position to define it more precisely. Although, whatever we call it, we can ultimately only infer the nature of the power inherent in a vision, or what it is in a revelation that releases such energy, the very process of attempting to delimit the

[1] *Sargant.*   [2] *Koestler.*   [3] *Weber.*

relevant operational fields brings us that much nearer to a more accurate assessment of the prophet, the revelation, the millennium itself, the diffuse form of the second phase of the cycle, and the way in which seemingly random activities cohere into a movement.

By regarding the overt and positive features of a movement as merely indicative of a far wider and more complex problem, as epiphenomenal, an 'Hegelian' explanation need not account for the negative instance. Nor does it have to explain why a movement took place precisely when it did. Being epiphenomenal, the activities signal a problem but are not in themselves the problem. The diffuse form of the second phase of the cycle here assumes a greater importance. For, lacking both prophet and a coherent movement, we are still provided with the indicators of a continuing and developing problem. We recognize these activities as pointing to a millenarian problem because we regard them as epiphenomenal. The prophet himself is epiphenomenal—as any true prophet would be the first to admit. He does not speak for himself, on his own account. He is 'spoken through'. He is the vehicle through which 'God', 'divine providence', the 'Spirit of History', or other kinds of divine powers communicate themselves to the society at large. Charisma, it becomes clear, is objectively defined by the kinds of acceptance accorded to the revelation. This is why some prophets are personal nonentities, why the organizer of a movement is not necessarily the prophet, and why, because they happen also to be politically competent, some prophets become heroes and political leaders. Charismatic qualities attach to the message rather than to the prophet. Nevertheless, if the prophet is able the message and the prophet may become closely identified. Charisma attaches to the prophet with an acceptable message. By defining any particular feature of a millenarian movement in terms of the relations between other features, a logical set of relations that is largely independent of narrative and chronology may be obtained.

An 'Hegelian' explanation is 'open-ended'. It enforces an appreciation of the total situation in which a millenarian movement takes place and is investigated. We begin to see that we are not dealing with the contingencies of particular economic events, or with a transient colonialism, or with lone individuals who happen to be deprived of established roles in community. We are analysing a broader historical process. From such a point of view a millenarian movement which attracts the attentions of a few hundred people cannot seem other than epiphenomenal, eddies in the stream. In this light the ethnographic details of the series of movements that have occurred in the Madang District of New Guinea, or which took place among the Plains Indians, become susceptible to sociological formulation. Accepting millenarian movements as epiphenomenal, an investigator is forced into perspectives far broader than those of the movements themselves. By entering into the broad stream of historical development, by recognizing the *gestalt*—that field of developing relations which is presently assuming a well-defined shape[1]—one may distinguish sets of competing assumptions, analyse the exploitation, distribution and allocation of material resources, and understand the relevance of the content of the millennium. Once such a developing situation is accepted, the formula thesis-antithesis-synthesis comes ready-made. Further, given that the logical contraries should correspond with the real contradictions and conflicts of life and the pragmatic experience, we are provided with a tool which enables us to penetrate differences of cultural idiom.

The advantages of an 'Hegelian' type of explanation or rationalization of the action are accompanied by pitfalls which are perhaps less obvious. The temptation to dwell on the prophet and so come to regard him as something more than human, as some kind of mystical embodiment of the historical process, is a strong one. Admitting the existence of operational powers which may be provisionally identified and explored from the standpoint of the known is one thing. Explaining the known in terms of the unknown is quite another. Since the epiphenomena make up the vast bulk of the known evidence, it is silly to ignore it in the attempt to speculate more nobly on the nature of the phenomenon. The comparatively tiny but very real world of those involved in a millenarian movement tends to be lost in a wide sweep of developmental universals. It is useful to remember that there is in millenarian movements just that vital and generative spark to which we owe our being as human, moral, and civilized. Reducing this spark to the abstract and mechanical is

[1] Compare *Wallace.*

a fault to which most kinds of explanation are only too prone.
And when we do this we must know we are wrong.

We may sum up and reformulate the kinds of explanation
considered in the following way:

1. Explanation by reference to assumptions about human
   nature in terms of:
   (a) Intuitive insights into human nature.
   (b) The special or more generalized folk-wisdoms of par-
       ticular sections of 'western' society.
   (c) Specific and systematic universes of discourse, whether
       biological or psychological.
2. Explanation in terms of the social conditions obtaining in
   a particular and relevant region in terms of:
   (a) The specific relations between groups or categories of
       persons.
   (b) The intellectual or philosophical or theological tradi-
       tions of the peoples concerned.
   (c) Positively orientated welfare politico-economics.
   (d) Historical narrative.
3. Explanation by reference to millennial views on the meaning of society and history in terms of:
   (a) Christian transcendentalisms.
   (b) Dialectical materialism.
4. Explanation by reference to views on the nature of human
   progress and development in terms of historical transcen-
   dentalism.
5. Explanation by reference to a variety of combinations of
   the above.

11
Explanation (ii)

The difficulties which lie in the way of classifying millenarian activities seem to spring from two main sources: the variety of kinds of explanation available, and the nature of the activities themselves. In spite of repeated pleas for classification, most scholars have been content with loose descriptive terms, making such *ad hoc* distinctions as might seem useful to them for particular purposes. On the whole the more popular appellations of particular periods and places—such as enthusiastic and cargo—have sufficed. Nor is this wholly surprising. Millenarists want to change everything, their activities are holistic, almost larger than life. They draw observers, investigators and bystanders into their orbits. Evidence and explanation and author become mutually involved. While parts of a movement may yield to this or that kind of explanation, the activities as wholes can only be fully understood within the terms of another and wider holism. An appropriate kind of holism is precisely what we presently lack.

Essentially, millenarian activities repeat in a variety of idioms the process whereby an animal became man, a moral being aware of his morality. They recapitulate the neolithic revolution, they trace the pattern of all those revolutions by which one kind of human condition, one mode of measuring the moral stature of man, is replaced by another in more complex circumstances. The main theme is moral regeneration: the generation of new moralities, the creation of a new man defined in relation to more highly differentiated criteria. The process involves the creation of new unities, a new community, a new set of assumptions within terms of which men and women may exploit the resources of their environment and order their relations with one another. Traditional man, isolated perhaps, but still living within the terms of a traditional order and set of assumptions, no longer suffices. Faced with relations which the traditional categories of understanding can no longer render intelligible, fresh categories are sought. Faced with experiences and kinds of behaviour which the traditional categories can no longer predict, whose ordering the traditional categories and assumptions can no longer guarantee, heart and mind plunge into the past to seek that inspiration which will carry them forward into new syntheses.

Most millenarian movements attract a variety of enthusiasts. Whether we call them 'misguided' or 'saintly' or 'charlatans' depends on how far our particular assumptions allow us to posit differing levels of awareness in others. Again, though it may be said that envy and covetousness, or greed and hate rather than a fiery love of one's fellows, inform many millenarian movements, this does not detract from the force of the general statement concerning new assumptions. But it draws attention to the differing viewpoints of particular authors. For where one may see envy and greed and hate, another may see dispossession, deprivation and exploitation. Similar situations are given quite different slants. Then there is the situation where, starting with new assumptions about the measure of man, a millenarian movement may end up by adopting the traditional and established measures which are too strong to overthrow. If a change-over of roles takes place, those who formerly objected to the way they were treated now mete out the same treatment to those whom they have displaced. Still, even if all that has been shown is that the bearers of a particular tradition were too weak to sustain it, and have yielded to others with the will and capacity to carry it forward into the future, the new assumptions were there at the start.

He who is powerful, rich and highly placed, or who is wedded to the appropriateness of a hierarchical ordering of society, can often afford to be charitable. Still, he tends to see a millenarian movement as a challenge to the power and authority of the established order. Whether as onlooker or investigator, his attitude towards a millenarian movement is coloured by his own convictions. Conversely, in a culture founded in principle on equality before God or the law, an egalitarian always has a groundswell of opinion in his favour. But whether as reporter or participant he is rarely untouched by envy or bitterness, and cannot but show a bias in favour of a change in the distribution of power. Between the confirmed believer in hierarchy and the convinced egalitarian lies a variety of compromise vocabularies, each of which, in describing and analysing the conditions in which millenarian movements have their genesis, tends to reflect the moral standpoint of author or investigator. Nor is the dilemma of one kind of morality sitting in judgement on another resolved by taking refuge in moral relativism. What seems to be needed in some way of saying something useful about millenarian activities that is not necessarily coloured by the adoption of a particular moral attitude towards them.

SITUATIONS AND OPPOSITIONS

At the start of this essay religion was regarded as a set of assumptions about power. And we have regarded millenarian activities as mainly concerned with the ordering and re-ordering of power. We must, therefore, isolate those situations in which power so manifests itself as to call for new assumptions about it. What we propose is a series of building blocks which can be used to construct the parts of a millenarian movement. For some activities only a few of these blocks will be necessary. Others may use the whole set.

Let us begin with four primary situations:

   (i) The 'aircraft situation', as exemplified by those New Guinea people who engaged in millenarian type activities on the sighting of an aircraft: millenarian activities occasioned by the manifestation of a power outside current comprehensions.

  (ii) The 'money situation': the question of an appropriate measurement of man, of how the qualities may be quantified by money, of the opposition between binary qualities and factorial quantities.

 (iii) The 'Brahman-Kshatriya situation', as exemplified in the discussion on the beginnings of Jainism: competition for, and the passage from one category to another of, known power or powers.

 (iv) The 'Plains Indians situation': new assumptions elicited by the complete physical defeat of a culture and way of life by another.

The first of these four situations is contained in some way in all millenarian movements or activities, the second and third in most, and the fourth in only a few. Not necessarily mutually exclusive, the four situations merely represent distinct types of situation which may call for a millenarian movement. They may also be broken down and recombined in terms of a series of oppositions. And to determine the axis of these oppositions we can conveniently turn to money. For although almost any manifestation of power outside current comprehensions may occasion millenarian activities, money and how to control and order it are the features which seem *most frequently* to call for new assumptions about power. On the one hand human beings tend to think in terms of contrary qualities or binary oppositions; on the other hand money, the concrete symbols of a factorial mathematical system, evokes the quite different and even opposed idea of the unbifurcated unity, the one-and-the-many. Given money as the determining axis, then, we may list some generally corresponding oppositions as follows:

A known and ordered environment	(1)	The advent of an unknown and unordered power
Quality	(2)	Number
Qualitative measures of man	(3)	Quantitative measures of man
Binary differentiation	(4)	Factorial differentiation
Reciprocity	(5)	Non-reciprocity
Part-time specialization	(6)	Full-time specialization
Treasure articles	(7)	Money
Subsistence economy	(8)	Complex economy
Political power based on segmentary oppositions	(9)	Political power based on superiority-inferiority
Shared values with equal access to rewards	(10)	Shared values with privileged access to rewards
Egalitarian or binary distributions of power	(11)	Power distributed between the prophet (one) and others (many)
Polytheism	(12)	Monotheism

The series of oppositions above constitute further blocks from which it seems possible to build up our four situations and most millenarian movements. Three features taken from the right-hand series have special shapes: money (7); the Brahman-

Kshatriya, which we abstract from (10); and the prophet (11). They will be considered in more detail presently. Meanwhile, though somewhat crude, the series of oppositions seems to hold good. They guide rather than insist. The vertical columns do not necessarily imply mutually exclusive sets. And though the features in either vertical column will tend to go together, each opposition is primarily an entity on its own, and of course the concrete situation will almost inevitably include features from both columns. Thus it is possible that a society with a complex economy (right hand (8)) will also have shared values with equal access to rewards (left hand (10); and a society guided by Number (right hand (2)) may also have developed ideas on Quality (left hand (2)). Nevertheless, the principle of opposition, and therefore of potential conflict, remains. They are opposites or oppositions. All that is being suggested is that in societies where the left-hand series is dominant, money (say) will evoke some of the features in the right-hand column, thus giving rise to a lively engagement between the values denoted by the relevant oppositions. Similarly, in societies where the right-hand series is dominant, questions on the proper use of money (say) will tend to evoke the comparative simplicities of the left-hand column. We are not saying that the engagement of one opposition will necessarily engage all. We are simply suggesting that the engagement of one or more of the series of oppositions seems to constitute the *mise en scène* of a millenarian movement, that by using some or all of these oppositions we can build a coherent model of a millenarian movement.

We can turn now to consider money, the Brahman-Kshatriya, and the prophet. In the course of discussion we shall see more clearly how the four situations and the twelve oppositions can be used.

MONEY

The advent of money into a society that previously had no money does not necessarily trigger off a millenarian movement. Nor in a money-using society does a millenarian movement always hinge on money. If millenarian activities can be occasioned by the flight of an aircraft over New Guinea, it is clear that money is not the only feature driving people to find new

kinds of explanation. Nevertheless, money seems to be the most
frequent and *convenient* axis on which millenarian movements
turn. Money points up the difference between qualitative and
quantitative measures of man in relation to his moral stature.
Money is significant in the colonial situation, and in the collision
between a subsistence and complex economy. We have seen
how, in the Jain example, the political bosses of a moneyed
economy can turn to management of finance. Money *is* wealth.
It retains its value through several generations, and inde-
pendently of a prescribed mode of access it may obtain prestige
and command. Because money used as money and not as a
treasure article is a basic measure of man, it allows of full-time
specialization. In turn, full-time specialization entails a further
differentiation of the qualities of man. Taking to their specialist
tasks, lone individuals seek association in terms of the further
differentiations of which they have now become aware, and they
search for the assumptions which will guarantee the validity of
their new-found qualities. As the handling of money habituates
its users to the notion of units composed of numbers of units,
the one-and-the-many, so in their experience of social life do
lone individuals and specialists in association become aware of
other lone individuals and other kinds of specialists. This provides an experience of 'manyness' on the one hand, and of the
unitary on the other.

It is important to distinguish between the unit conceived as a
pair of complementary halves, and the unit conceived as one.
In the former case we are dealing with a system of binary opposites, and in the latter with a factorial system in which, though
the idea of one is fixed, each convenient unit is divisible into an
infinite series of parts. In the millenarian situation the prophet is
a single whole individual in whom the several threads of a social
and historical experience meet. An unbifurcated unity—which
may, however, consist of parts—as distinct from a unity that
may be broken into contraries is also fixed in the notion of
explicit monotheism, a single and unbifurcated source of power
which may nevertheless consist of parts. And it is precisely an
awareness of this that, in the colonial situation for example,
Christian missionaries set out to make quite plain. No longer a
combination of theses and antitheses, synthesis begins to be
seen as something *sui generis*, as something quite different from,

and larger than, the sum of the parts which comprise it. If in a traditional scheme there is an implicit idea of the unity that cannot itself be broken down into contraries, making the notion explicit seems to release energies hitherto dormant. Those habituated to a dominant scheme of binary contraries attempt to differentiate further, attempt to come to grips with the one-and-the-many. Conversely, where the idea of the unbifurcated unity is traditional and explicit, as in the Christian tradition, the idea of wholeness as one and a multiplicity becomes sharply opposed to the binary scheme. The interplay between the two schemes corresponds with, or begets, doubt and anxiety. The millenarian situation in the traditionally moneyed community reveals attempts to re-order what seems to have become an unmanageable manyness into sharply contrasted contraries. Life is so multifaceted, so to speak, that it becomes almost impossible to exercise that basic moral capacity, the discrimination between right and wrong. The solution to this is a reformulation into contraries. And the rigorisms of European millenarian movements—where the elect are distinguished from the damned as white from black—instance this process most clearly. But it is, I think, characteristic of all millenarian movements. A scheme of binary contraries is required if those who join are to be sharply distinguished from those who do not.

Though the idea of the 'many' seems implicit in all human thought and experience, the idea of 'oneness' is uncomfortable. It goes against the grain of most of social experience. It tends to break down, to be laid aside or re-rationalized into binary contraries. Yet it remains that the fact or idea of an unbifurcated unity, oneness or singularity, exists. And men seem compelled to give it expression, explain it, and come to terms with it.[1] Oneness or the singular are repugnant both to the moral sense and a moral order. For while the moral engagement of human relationships must imply forms of reciprocity, pairings,

---

[1] The idea of singularity or unbifurcated oneness is sometimes symbolized by primitive peoples in the penis or vulva. Each consists of parts, and, except by cutting (circumcision, subincision, both of which are symbols of socialization in that they symbolically bifurcate, thus signalling the moral condition) there is no sense in which either organ can be bifurcated into contraries. Further, the penis is juxtaposed with two testicles (the singular and the pair); and a woman's breasts stand in a corresponding relation to the vulva.

and the binary discrimination between right and wrong actions, the idea of oneness tends to place the self not in a context of pairings, in a community defined by inter-relatedness, but to evoke the single unique individual among many others: a basic conflict between social personality or category and the unique individual. Accepting that missionaries nurture an awareness of the one-and-the-many and the individual, the handling of money brings this awareness into the realm of the concrete, into the conduct of day-to-day relations. And by doing so it negates the primacy of the pairings in order to make sense of the one-and-the-many. Such manifestations of oneness and the singular as, for example, the sorcerer, the professional killer, the non-conformist, the tyrant, sickness and death, demonstrate in an everyday way that reciprocities, the basic foundation of man's morality to man, are but an imposition on a reality that is quite otherwise. Experiences of the singular in such ways may provoke men into attempting to come to terms with the idea of oneness. But against this one must set the far larger and more usual experience of reciprocities in day-to-day relations with others. On the other hand, manipulated every day, permanently in the forefront of awareness, money is a concrete representation of the one-and-the-many. It creates relationships, may vitiate, break, ennoble or enforce them. Money lends itself to non-reciprocal action.

On account of its keeping qualities, money may draw out the historical sense by evoking a sense of time as a developing continuum with a beginning and end. In a subsistence economy time is usually conceived as a cyclical continuum, determined by the life cycle, ecology and kin categories.[1] Moreover, virtue tends to be contained in the nature of things, grows out of the organization of the skills and industry necessary to survival itself, is virtually enforced by the implications of maintaining the community. In the looser and more highly differentiated complex society with money, virtue becomes much more a matter of choice. The nature of man may be ennobled or degraded in an almost infinite variety of ways. In the sense that one act of virtue may undo a number of defects held in a past reputation, the aphorism that time is money gains an added significance. Millenarists find in the closed community the soil

[1] See for an example *Evans-Pritchard* (1), pp. 94–138.

in which virtues can flower, and in the relatively open society that jungle of opportunity where vices proliferate like weeds. And though the rigorisms and tight conformities characteristic of the relatively closed community tend to go together with witchcrafts and sorceries, the evil-doer can the more easily be identified (or created and then identified) and extirpated. As the tight organization breeds its particular and manifest virtues, so transgressions become the more obvious. But money, belonging to the highly differentiated society whose ideas on virtue, vice, right and wrong are likewise highly complex and differentiated, demands greater freedom of choice, reveals the vice in cultivated virtues, allows no vice without some virtue, concedes an element of right in wrong-doing, finds the sin of pride in an upright fellow. Just these kinds of differentiation the millenarist in a moneyed society cannot abide.[1] The unordered emergence of just these kinds of differentiation in the non- or newly-moneyed community is what a millenarist seeks to control.

In requiring that virtue should grow from the will and capacity of the single individual rather than emerge from the secretions of a culturally determined and tightly buttressed social personality, money invites a complex differentiation and multiplication of the parts and qualities of man. Money, it is said, is the root of all evil. And in ways that the subsistence or relatively closed community cannot provide, money and the open society certainly offer an infinity of occasions on which to be evil. On the other hand money also offers the individual both the time and the opportunity to mould his nature in an image of all that is contained in the good. Tracing the lineaments of power, measuring and differentiating the capacities and powers of men and women, allowing them to be the authors of themselves, money, like the unbifurcated source of power it evokes, is in itself neutral, independent of the moralities as set forth by men. But because money is passive and can be used for a variety of ends, it vitiates the bundle of binary qualities on which a moral order is based. Money as an abstract, factorial and quantitative system must be opposed to the qualities that measure the stature of man. Yet it also evokes the individual in whom, ultimately, the highest qualities of being human are reckoned.

---

[1] Compare *Cohn*, as quoted above, pp. 120–1, and *Knox*, as cited on pp. 126–8.

THE BRAHMAN-KSHATRIYA RELATIONSHIP

In the simplest and most general sense the scene is set for a millenarian movement when men become aware of a power which they cannot understand, which their current assumptions cannot explain or validate. Further, men most often become aware that there is something they have to explain by means of new assumptions when they feel they must reconcile the kinds of conflict implied by the oppositions we have discussed above. In this, money is most often both catalyst and flux. It focuses the oppositions on a particular level of significance and compels the effort to synthesize. But if we are to appreciate at another level the operations involved in attempting a synthesis, we must use a different focus and see the series of oppositions through the lens of what we have called the Brahman-Kshatriya relationship.

This relationship is a triad:

(a) Two categories of person share the same hierarchy of values and assumptions about the nature of power and its proper distribution and use.

(b) Of these two categories one only (Brahman) has access to the rewards implied in holding the assumptions and values, and the other (Kshatriya) does not.

(c) Between them, Brahman and Kshatriya generate the *guru* or teacher or prophet.

The relationship is a triad; the generation of the prophet is 'built in'. A relationship that seems to satisfy the first two conditions, (a) and (b), but not the third (c), is another kind of relationship. Our interest, specifically, lies in the triad. While we shall continue to use the Indian terms, the labels 'Brahman', 'Kshatriya', and *'guru'* or prophet are to be thought of as categories by means of which a general relationship may be examined.

The Brahman, then, has an exclusive access to the rewards implied in the assumptions which he holds in common with the Kshatriya. Only the Brahman may gain redemption. No matter how he acts the Kshatriya cannot gain the same redemption. Such a dyadic relationship may continue for generations. What interests us is what can happen to the dyad to make it a triad. And the answer seems to be, a transmission of power from

Brahman to Kshatriya. While the commonly held hierarchy of values and assumptions still hold, it gradually becomes evident to the Kshatriyas that the Brahmans, maliciously or otherwise, have misinterpreted their common assumptions. Revering the Brahman, who specializes in his knowledge of the commonly held assumptions and values, the Kshatriya sits at his feet and learns from him until, almost the equal of the Brahman in knowledge, or more than his equal, he is able to think for himself: the power inherent in the knowledge of the Brahman passes to the Kshatriya, or becomes equally divided between Brahman and Kshatriya. The Kshatriyas are in a position to teach themselves and to transmit the power of learning between themselves. At this point the Kshatriya who is as learned as the Brahman takes it upon himself to do some research on his own. He delves into tradition, can find no issue of principle in which he essentially differs from the Brahman, and says so. The *guru* or prophet—in embryo at least—has been generated: it remains to widen the breach until the old assumptions, rechannelled into new action implications, begin to look like new assumptions. In the course of time they become new assumptions.

The significant feature here is not so much the exclusive access to redemption, but the transmission of power from Brahman to Kshatriya. The time-scale through which the process of transmission takes place varies greatly. Not until a prophet has been generated can it be known that—from the point of view of the Brahman—too much power has been transmitted. When a prophet has been generated the oppositions, (5), (9), (10) and (11) are engaged. A non-reciprocal relationship is becoming more nearly reciprocal; a more equal distribution of power is resulting in a rough balance of opposed forces; power based on superiority–inferiority—or rulers and ruled—is becoming nullified; and the egalitarian or binary distribution of power begins to move over to the figure of the prophet, eliciting the one-and-the-many. At this point a millenarian movement might, but need not, occur. What is important is that the generation of the prophet is not simply dependent on a permissive political regime, or on a relationship between privileged and underprivileged. It goes with a transmission of power from one category to another.

The Melanesian scene provides a concrete example. In this

case white men, more particularly the administration, are like Brahmans; and the Melanesians become like Kshatriyas.[1] Power is in the hands of the whites. White men have guns, money, goods, knowledge, techniques of various kinds. Gradually, however, power begins to flow towards the Melanesians. They are useful, they do a variety of tasks, the administration and other whites begin to depend on them. To make them even more useful and dependable the Melanesians are taught new ways, trained in new techniques. Missionaries build schools and teach their charges mathematical, literary and technological skills as well as the values of monotheism, love, and a brotherhood in Christ. European traders with goods and money give this teaching a practical component. Melanesians gain experience in the handling of money, begin to recognize the series of virtues and vices that goes together with a more differentiated awareness. Formerly faced with packaged virtues which lead on to influence and status on the one hand, and vices which lead to exclusion or death on the other, they are now confronted with a series of single choices each of which implies some virtue and some vice, and none of which necessarily leads on to a worthwhile status. Moral Europeans,[2] whether missionaries or administrative officers or others, treat Melanesians on a level of equality and give the impression that powers have indeed been equalized. But as the Melanesians begin to share in the same hierarchy of values as the whites—monotheism and the values attaching to money and the deployment of manufactured goods—so do they begin to realize that the whites have an exclusive access to the rewards of what are believed to be commonly held assumptions. Money comes into the hands of the Melanesians only to trickle through them and pile up in the houses of the whites. Though Melanesians have access to a variety of cheap trinkets, the more valuable stuffs are for whites only; only white men are in positions of authority valid for the total environment. Now, whether the Melanesians are thought of as covetous, or as imbued with a passionate desire for moral equality, the objective fact is that power has flowed from white

[1] Millenarian activities immediately following on first contacts are 'aircraft situations': something has occurred and needs to be explained. With circumstances such as these we can go no further than we have done, for lack of further evidence.   [2] Above, pp. 67–9.

to Melanesian, from Brahman to Kshatriya. At this point the generation of a prophet indicates that there are some who believe that this power is becoming equalized. All twelve oppositions may be engaged.

Each of our four primary situations ultimately envisages the emergence of a prophet. The fact that a passage of power from one locus to another is contained in all four of them does not make it any the less useful to keep them distinct. In the 'aircraft situation' the extent and content of the power that might be transferred is unknown to the people, and the source of power to be manipulated is only approximately and imprecisely defined. In the 'Plains Indians situation' a transference of power is being sought from two sources: from tradition as well as from the conquerors. But, as the revelations of the different prophets show, precisely what kinds of power are being sought from either source is not clear. The 'money situation' implies the transference of financial power: on the one hand a command over goods and labour, on the other a means of quantifying and factorializing the qualities. But, unlike the Brahman who is a category of person who is malleable and who has known powers, money is as impervious to persuasion and moral pressures as thunder or lightning.

The Brahman-Kshatriya is only one of several ways in which a prophet may be generated. Nevertheless, because it refers to identifiable categories of persons, it is a useful model which can be applied to most millenarian movements. It focuses attention on the generation of a prophet in circumstances determined by the transference of power where both sides are agreed on what the main assumptions are, and where the transferrers have been enjoying an exclusive access to the rewards implied in the shared assumptions.

THE PROPHET

So much has been written about prophets[1] that it may seem unnecessary to write more. But since the four primary situations imply the ultimate emergence of prophets, and prophets

---

[1] Everything written about millenarian movements contains something about prophets. But no anthropologist can go very wrong by referring first to *Evans-Pritchard* (3), pp. 287–310, and then to *Emmet*.

are the key to millenarian *movements* as distinct from the diffuse *activities* we have discussed,[1] we should say something about them. While the four situations and the twelve oppositions enable us to construct generalized models of most millenarian activities, the figure of the prophet needs greater specificity. Because the prophet manifests an accretion of power, drawing him more sharply will also clarify the situations and oppositions.

We tend to take prophets for granted. But should we? They are dangerous people. In what senses are they necessary? We know of no prophets in nature, and far from being essential to the survival of human groups their appearances in particular instances has often seemed disastrous. On the other hand, given the ways in which prophets articulate new assumptions, it becomes difficult to see how else such assumptions could be articulated. If we consider what is implied by, say, new assumptions being articulated by a committee, we find at once that we are begging just those questions raised by millenarian activities. We presuppose an adherence to established usage. We presuppose precisely that kind of order which a millenarian movement is trying to create. We presuppose just that comprehension of available power to which the movement appears to aspire.[2]

We know of no societies which lack shamans, diviners or seers or the like. But not all communities are familiar with the prophet. A prophet carries the interpretative role of the diviner out of an established framework into a quite new ambience of awareness. Though, therefore, we cannot say that a prophet is a necessary feature of the general human condition, there are particular moments—our situations and oppositions—when he may become necessary. On account of our own millenarian traditions we are prone to accept the periodic appearances of prophets as rather less remarkable than the appointment of a new prime minister. It takes an effort of the imagination to appreciate his impact on a culture wholly unfamiliar with the emergence of prophets. Yet it is just this effort of informed and calculated imagination that we must invoke if we are to account

[1] Above, pp. 57–9.

[2] Over the last few years, since New Guineans have been given the opportunity to do committee work within an ordered framework, and to elect their own representatives, the incidence of cargo cults has markedly decreased. See also below, p. 172, n. 1.

for the appearance of a prophet anywhere. A singular person among many ordinary folk, a prophet is in himself an image of the one-and-the-many, the situation predicated by money. Although he may not himself collect cash subscriptions—few prophets are inclined to render unto Caesar the things that are Caesar's—much of what a prophet has to say hinges on the handling of money. Either he tries to make money a relevant measure of man, or he denies that money can measure anything but itself.

A prophet is generally believed to have access to a source of inspiration that transcends man's ordinary wits. He either symbolizes the new man in himself, or he is the vehicle by means of which the lineaments of the new man may become known. He imposes certainty on a situation characterized by doubts. He must articulate thoughts and aspirations and emotions that are immanent in the community to which he speaks if he is to be acceptable as a prophet. He externalizes and articulates what it is that others can as yet only feel, strive towards and imagine but cannot put into words or translate explicitly into action. Would-be prophets, of whom a community takes little notice, or rejects, do not appropriately put into words what members of the community feel; or do not in themselves project a satisfactory image of the new man. At any rate, acceptability does not necessarily depend on soft words well spoken. The authoritative voice may speak harshly, or sternly. It may promise preliminary hardships or comforts; it may plead or condemn, castigate, encourage or nag. Still, it commands an audience.

Whence comes this authority, and how may it be recognized? Divine inspiration of one kind or another is certainly one criterion. And if we say that charismatic qualities are necessary we merely restate the question. How can one explain a false prophet whose divine revelation appears as otherwise impeccable? To speak of his 'timing' is to beg the question. Most prophets are amateurs who make the kind of mistakes which today's professional persuaders associate with amateurism. Still, since the unorthodox is often the seed from which a new orthodoxy springs, a prophet's 'mistakes' are often fertile mistakes which move men to action in circumstances where the professional fails. Yet if there are men and women who set out to become prophets, no prophet may be thought of as selecting

his moment. He is 'spoken through'. The revelation comes, is
articulated. The spark may fall on dry tinder and burst into
flame, or it may glow for a moment and die in the dark. On the
other hand, the very facts that a prophet is 'spoken through',
but that not all prophets who are clearly and obviously 'spoken
through' are equally effective, point to implicit criteria of relevance. Accepting that the effective revelation cannot be wholly
accounted for, there are special circumstances in particular
cases which contribute towards the selection of one kind of man
rather than another,[1] and it is still possible to adduce certain
general features which seem to lend a prophet authority, and
which go some way towards determining the bases of charisma.

The first clear point is that the divine inspiration should be
gained in traditional terms.[2] However silly or obtuse, the revelation which is gained in a traditional way has authenticity and is
accorded a hearing. True, once heard it may be rejected. Still, it
may trigger a series of activities which gradually come under the
control of others with different revelations, or it may provide
the necessary basis of experience for accepting a later revelation. It is always worth listening to, and in the millenarian
ambience always worth thinking about. Then there is the personal experience of the prophet himself in the total situation.
For though, initially, it is the revelation which triggers a movement, and revelations often come through quite odd persons,
revelations with staying power tend to be transmitted by particular kinds of person. In Oceania, for example, the vast
majority of effective prophets have had a relatively wide
experience of the white man's world. It is true that some
Oceanic prophets with a slender experience of the Europeanized
environment—but with a vivid imagination of what the white
man's world must be like, perhaps—have initiated effective
millenarian movements. But these are few. Most of them have
been mission teachers, men selected on account of their charac-
ter and qualities of intellect, and then given a special training
denied to others. They have usually been well travelled men,

---

[1] *Burridge* (3), pp. 254–66, where the prophet was effective because
he was a stranger, an outsider.

[2] Further research may show that there have been effective prophets
with revelations gained in non-traditional ways. But it is not going to
be easy to show a non-traditional way.

who have rubbed shoulders with all sorts and sizes in the hurly-
burly of the greater commercial community. Relatively expert
in the handling of money, they have begun to think more
effectively in quantitative terms. They have encountered, or
been taught, explicit monotheism. They are also men for whom
a traditional and explicit ordering of the relations of daily life in
terms of binary opposites has become merged in the experience
of the multiplicity of individual things and persons-in-them-
selves.

With some appreciation of the diversity of tasks and jobs to
be found in the greater community, the Oceanic prophets of
whom we speak have been those who have begun to see the
advantages of specialization, differentiated criteria of status,
and complex forms of organization. They have also been men
who have so grown in awareness that they are able to be in-
formedly critical of these conditions. To their own communities
if not to Europeans, they have been men whose general
acquaintance with the wider environment and larger community is evidence of the fact that they can understand it and
cope with it. In themselves, that is, not only are they new men,
symbolizing the new man, but they may speak with authority
because, drawing strength from the 'moral European', they do
indeed approximate those who habitually wield authority. Conversely, as has been demonstrated elsewhere,[1] a European who
has become sufficiently involved in the native way of life so as
to appear to exhibit the same characteristics or 'mixture' as a
New Guinean who has become involved in the European way of
life, may himself be greeted as a minor prophet. Yet all this is
but to spell out within the terms of a particular situation the
general Brahman-Kshatriya relationship. To come nearer home,
for example, in relation to his followers John Wesley exhibited
much the same features as Oceanic prophets to their followers.[2]
Like Yali, Wesley was born of impoverished parents with a large
family to support, and he became identified with a class of
persons which had been virtually disenfranchized and denied
the rewards offered by society and the established church. Still,
like Yali, Wesley made a breakthrough. He was educated by
those in power, and he became accepted by the privileged class
as one who had the same knowledge and ability as themselves.

[1] *Burridge* (3), p. 7.   [2] *Sargant.*

But, when the transference of power was complete, he was disowned because he used his knowledge for unorthodox ends. Nevertheless, in showing how access to power might be gained, Wesley, like Yali, symbolized the new way of life which he offered to his followers.

It is true that there are occasions when people will follow a leader more stupid and narrow but more confident and certain than themselves. But the social as distinct from the psychological conditions of confidence presuppose a wider and more informed experience. No one follows a lesser man. The leaders in the activities from which we have taken our 'aircraft situation' must be supposed to have been thought more capable than others. They tried to show their fellows how to enlarge their traditional assumptions about power so that the intrusion of an aircraft into their world could be made intelligible. The Christian elements in the revelations of Plains Indian prophets show them to have had a wider articulate experience than their fellow clansmen. But why a wider experience should lead to that divine and acceptable revelation which bestows charisma and authority is not easy to demonstrate. Because this is what most often happens it seems 'natural' that it should happen. But this begs the question, and it is worthwhile considering the point.

When prophets attempt to explain themselves and their experience, knowledge and thoughts to their fellows—which every traveller or explorer, whether he has been exploring lands or ideas, likes to do—they must use the language of those whom they wish to convert, persuade, chide or enliven. They are forced to explain the greater in terms of the smaller; they have to explain an experience in an idiom which does not contain it. They can only speak of 'wonders' which they may have experienced but which their audience has not and must take on faith.[1] Now while it is sometimes said that the more 'blind faith' is called for, the more it is freely given, most people are less ingenuous and demand a surer basis for their faith. They call for signs and proofs, attempt in pragmatic ways to test the authenticity of the prophet.[2] Behind the appearance of 'blind faith' there are often securely based motives for action. For example, when Joseph Smith's three most intimate disciples

[1] *Burridge* (3), pp. 196–202.　　　　[2] *Burridge* (3).

demanded to see the book of golden tablets on which their leader had based his revelation, Smith took the doubters into his house to show them the tablets. And when the disciples complained they could see nothing, Smith rounded on them with 'O ye of little faith! Kneel and pray—then you will see them!'[1] And see the tablets they did. That there was much to be lost in not seeing them, and a whole new world to be won if indeed they were seen, is not necessarily cynical.

Aladdin,[2] we are told, ventured forth and came to a high, dark cave. He went inside and found there jewels and gold past counting. He also found a dusty, traditional lamp which he thought he would clean and brighten. A genie appeared, holding the promise of all that heart and mind could desire.

In just such a way does a prophet go out of his world to enter a cavern of experience. Sometimes he finds a dusty old lamp which, with a little spit and a rub, may bring forth a genie. But like Aladdin he has to be careful. When his back is turned the old lamp and its genie may be traded for a bright new lamp without a genie. Without the genie a prophet's revelation is apt to be just another tall story.

A prophet is an adventurer, and his revelation often bears the hallmarks of any traveller's tale. Yet somewhere between interestedness, simple disbelief and blind faith a prophet with a genie will find a point in which interests, faith and degrees of belief or disbelief are brought into a fruitful union. This may have something to do with shock,[3] and for the prophet himself as well as for his audience there may be a bisociative jolt:[4] features, hitherto thought unrelated because comprehended in quite distinctive contexts, may suddenly appear related and beget a context of relatedness. Every anthropologist has experienced 'culture shock': a temporary inability, when moving from one culture to another, to grasp and act and think in terms of the assumptions upon which the newly entered culture is based. Not only is this shock experienced in fieldwork, while one

---

[1] *Fulop-Miller*, pp. 95–6.

[2] The name, which can be transliterated from the Arabic as *'Allā' al Din.* breaks down into *Alā*, height, on high, and *addīn*, religion (supplied).

[3] Cf. *Sargant*, Ch. 1.

[4] Cf. *Koestler*, pp. 35 ff.

learns the ways of a new culture, but it is experienced even more disconcertingly when one returns to one's own culture. Mind and emotions are confused; two different worlds have met in the same person. One alternative is insanity. Another is to comprehend one world in the terms of the other.

In this restricted sense every anthropologist has some share in the experience of a prophet, and every prophet must have something of the anthropologist in him. Both must pare their experiences into what is communicable. An anthropologist is trained to appreciate just this shift from one mode of thought to another. Nevertheless, in the event he is never quite ready for it. How much the greater, then, is the shock and turmoil in one who is not wholly aware of the nature of the transition in which he is involved?

> If thou hadst not gone out nor heard no tidings thou wouldst the better have abided in peace; and since it delighteth thee sometimes to hear new tidings it behoveth, following this, that thou suffer turbation of heart.[1]

If it seems likely that a prophet will be found acceptable because he is expected, we have to remember that a good deal of European history has been fashioned by prophets who were rejected by those who were supposed to be expecting them. The ancient mariner was entirely unexpected, even unwanted and repugnant. But he held his audience with his eye. Again, though the Mahdi might have had the 'look of a redeemer, being a man of tall stature, with black and gleaming eyes, and a fascinating gap between his upper incisor teeth',[2] it is perhaps rather to what à Kempis' translator calls 'turbation of heart'— that compulsion to communicate a particular kind of experience—that we should look if we are to account for the Mahdi's persuasiveness. For though in his personal appearance the Mahdi fitted extant expectations as to what a prophet should look like, without his genie and driving ambition it may fairly be doubted whether anyone would have given him a second glance.

Like other prophets, the Mahdi was found to be extremely attractive to women. So much so that his divine mission was laid aside and he became a libertine. No doubt the Mahdi's

[1] *Thomas à Kempis*, p. 39 (Bk. 1, Ch. XX).
[2] *Fulop·Miller*, pp. 83–5.

sexual charms were considerable. But one may still note that in most societies, particularly within Islam, women constitute an underprivileged class. James Naylor, a brave and honest man, is surely more properly evaluated as a prophet in terms of the millenarian atmosphere that accompanied the victories of the Parliamentary armies—in which he had served and fought with distinction—than by the fact that women extolled the beauty of his eyes and found him sexually attractive.[1] Yali, perhaps the most successful and influential of Oceanic prophets to date, charged five shillings for his sexual favours and—ironic to relate—was eventually imprisoned on a charge of rape.

What is the significance of the commonly reported sexual attractions of prophets? Until recently there were few communities in which women were not simply home-makers and child-bearers. Apart from a privileged few, usually elderly and past the flushes of sexual enjoyment, women have played little part in the management of political affairs. They have been in the main uneducated in intellectual matters, untrained in public managerial techniques. Exchanged or bought in marriage, they have been regarded as chattels who followed their men and did what they were told. Interacting most significantly in the sexual act, the relations between men and women have been largely determined by the overt ordering of different kinds of sexual access. Even if she understood him, of what interest to a Sudanese peasant woman were the Mahdi's dreams of glory, the Caliphate and empire if not, surely, the privileged luxury and influence of being a member of his harem? And much the same may be said of the ladies of New Guinea, whose aspirations are largely realized in being the wife of a rich and important man. On the whole, therefore, the sexual attractiveness of male prophets is to be accounted for less in the amatory skills of the prophet, and more in the conditions of being of women. Not for nothing did Jupiter come to Danae in a shower of coins. A prophet offers both sexes a wider and more satisfying redemption, and his sexual attractions and virility suggest an awareness of new babies as well as new men: total rebirth, a new community.

Peculiarly seminal, a prophet is but human, perhaps more truly human than his fellows: a statement which bears upon the

[1] *Fulop-Miller*, p. 73; *Matthews*, pp. 3–42.

nature of charisma. Though no god was ever prophet, men are
as gods and a prophet is most godlike. It is not appropriate to
think of a prophet as reduced in size to a schizophrene or a
paranoid, someone mentally sick. In relation to those to whom
he speaks a prophet is necessarily corrupted by his wider
experience. He is an 'outsider', an odd one, extraordinary.
Nevertheless, he specifically attempts to initiate, both in himself as well as in others, a process of moral regeneration. Both
he and his audience are caught between opposed conditions of
being. But whereas the prophet has travelled some way along
the road towards the synthesis, and in himself represents it, his
audience has to be persuaded into taking the same path. As an
adventurer a prophet is by definition one who needs no guarantees outside his own resources. He deliberately places himself at
hazard, seeks the situation where survival depends on his own
faith, conviction, and qualities of initiative and perception. Continually exercised in self-reliance, in standing alone where others
habitually rely on kinsfolk or friends or neighbours or allies a
prophet is an individual-in-himself who points up the humanity
in man and also exhibits those qualities of the divine free-mover
to which all men at some times in their lives aspire. Yet a
prophet who asserted his lone singularity would not find himself
welcome or wanted. He must fulfill his uniqueness not as singular merely, but as a particularly intense expression of those
qualities which his audience regards as specifically fitting the
nature of man. Not singular in a way that will make him an
outcast, a prophet sees in himself all those to whom he speaks,
and they see themselves in him—a communion from which
charisma is surely born. Through this communion, perhaps, a
prophet comes to realize that although he requires no guarantees
outside of himself and his message, ordinary folk normally do.

Acceptable guarantees are part of charisma. People involved
in a millenarian movement take risks and are caught in the
dilemma of choice as they attempt to move from one moral
system to another. Whether the movement is gradual, as in the
Kekesi rites, or a quicker and more radical shift, as in most
millenarian movements, in addition to those who have nothing
to lose but their chains influential men are also involved. These
men, whose prestige in the community is based upon one set of
assumptions, have to choose between an established position of

power and a new mode of redemption about which they know little. Are such men as these being reckless, hoping against all experience for an even better deal, or are they attempting to come to terms with a moral order which they recognize as being wider or more meaningful than the traditional? Some participants in a millenarian movement may be motivated by prospects of greater material rewards, a wider field of action, a short-cut to success, or the excitement of fresh endeavours. But as participants they have to commit themselves publicly to accepting the assumptions which will guarantee and legitimize the greater rewards. Thus, though the rewards of accepting the assumptions may be as material as anyone could wish, the guarantees which a prophet provides should be, and generally are, of a moral and even mystical rather than material kind. If a prophet cannot touch, and so be sustained by, springs of moral awareness in his audience, his moment of glory will be brief.

We have come round full circle. If a prophet is to touch the springs of moral renewal, there must be an awareness of moral dilemma. And moral dilemma implies dissonances in basic assumptions about power. These, in turn, can be seen in stresses and strains in social relations, and are particularly expressed in the prestige system in terms of which the worth of man is measured, integrity earned, and redemption gained. We are now talking of the millenarian ambience from which millenarian activities are born. We are back to that quarrying into tradition whose purpose is to find those authentic principles which can be channelled anew. We have returned to that wider pragmatic experience which, fraught with contradictions, appears as the basis of the mystical experience through which new insights into man's condition of being may be obtained, and by virtue of which the prophet externalizes his experience in an attempt to define the new assumptions which will generate a new moral order.

We have attempted no holistic rationalization of the action involved in millenarian activities. Nor can we at present realize the suggestion (p. 104) that a classification of these activities should go to redemptive processes and syntheses. We need more detailed evidence of what happens in each of our primary situations, and we need a viable classification of socio-symbolic orders. On the other hand, we have offered some explanatory models. We have tried to show how the sets of relations indicated by the four primary situations and twelve oppositions enable us to build a coherent picture of millenarian activities. Accepting that these relations may be combined in a variety of ways, and that a particular movement need not require all of them, they provide us with the essential parts of a millenarian movement within a framework of loose possibilities and probabilities. We may sum up as follows:

(i) The issue is not whether different kinds of human being have different thought processes, but what often happens when, because of some event or series of events, there is a transference from one ambience of awareness to another, from one symbolic code or map to another, from one social order to another.

(ii) Usually but not always associated with extant competing moral systems and redemptive processes—and so bearing upon integrity and prestige—the transference entails widening comprehensions and an accretion of intellectual powers which tend to be translated into political and economic action.

(iii) Money, posing the problems of reconciling (a) binary discriminations with the differentiations entailed in the one-and-the-many, and (b) qualitative with quantitative and factorial measures of man, is the hinge on which most millenarian activities seem to turn.

(iv) The prophet, whose appearance gives millenarian activities the coherence of a movement, shows forth the contradictions of a particular social experience, posits solutions, and enables followers to define what they are or want to be.

To round off the picture we have to discuss the millennium as a thing-in-itself.

12
The Millennium

We have suggested that bereft of the millenarian ambience Yali would have been simply another capable man.[1] And the same could be said of most effective prophets. They are travellers and adventurers into new lands and ideas until, 'spoken through' and deriving charisma from the millenarian ambience, they fulfil themselves as prophets. Though they might be eccentric, outside the millenarian ambience few prophets would stand out from their fellows as singular men capable of doing so much. Logically, prophet, followers and activities belong to a framework of relevance generated by the meaning of the millennium. Hence the significance of the millennium as a thing-in-itself. What is it? What does it imply?

If we try to extricate ourselves from the purely Judaeo-Christian connotations of the millennium, it is fair to say that, in principle, the millennium is equivalent to salvation and to redemption itself.[2] Through and behind the variety of cultural idioms in which it may be expressed, the millennium points to a condition of being in which humans become free-movers, in which there are no obligations, in which all earthly desires are satisfied and therefore expunged. A new earth merges into the new heaven. On the other hand, the phraseology of millennial aspirations always envisages a new set of rules, new kinds of obligation, a new earth in which heaven is more brightly mirrored. Yet heaven and earth are distinct and opposed. And from this basic opposition between no rules and new rules, it would seem, there arises the transition process exemplified in various kinds of millenarian activity. Destruction of crops, livestock and other means of gaining a livelihood, through which men and women express and discharge their obligations to each other, represent or symbolize the millennium. No rules

[1] Above, p. 73.   [2] Above, p. 8.

are expressed in the lack of means for incurring obligations. No rules and new rules meet in the prophet who initiates the one whilst advocating the other.

The same dichotomy between no rules and new rules appears in many myths of origin. These tell of a golden age in which beings, not yet men and women, are free-movers and without rules. Then, often through a series of progressive stages in which awareness grows, these free-movers become men and women. And they do so at the point when an articulate awareness makes them subject to explicit rules. Pictured in a variety of ways, usually in relation to an awareness of the meanings of death and incest, 'moral awareness' and 'subjection to rules' are two sides of the same coin: the human condition. Between the gods and spirits and other free-movers, for whom in themselves morality is irrelevant, and the beasts and plants which are programmed with instincts and responses, lies man. He too is programmed. But he is also aware of himself, subject to rules which he thinks of as derived from a divine source, and which tell him the difference between right action and wrong.

Moral awareness implies rules, and different communities have their own particular rules by which they define their modes of morality. Yet in all transition rites there is a phase when those passing from one status to another, from one set of determinitive rules to another, are impliedly and temporarily subject to no rules at all.[1] The transient is separated off, placed apart until he can be inducted into a new set of rules. And this suspension of the human condition, a situation of 'no rules', appears as a necessary stage in the progression from 'old rules' to 'new rules'. The formula, old rules—no rules—new rules, fits our view of the thought and action of a millenarian movement. It also corresponds with the hegelian thesis-antithesis-synthesis. Nevertheless, a millenarian movement is a special kind of transition process. It is holistic, all embracing. In envisaging a quite new set of rules it recapitulates the process whereby an animal crossed the threshold to become man, and through which one sort of man becomes a new sort of man. Ordinary transitions occur within a more or less precisely formulated social order in which the three states are well known and defined. But when the social order itself is to be changed the

[1] See *Van Gennep*, pp. 65 ff.

new rules can only be experimental, approximately formulated.

The fact that millenarists are experimenting with new rules lends added point to the scenes of sexual promiscuity which accompany many of the movements. Copulation goes with revolution; virile prophets show their followers the way. As a particular expression of 'no rules', sexual promiscuity reiterates those first beginnings when there was no awareness of rules, when the first rules to be made ordered the conduct of sexual access by means of the incest taboo. And because the orgies of millenarian activities are engaged in *after* the participants have become roughly acquainted with the new rules, the implication is that before the new man can be realized a period of being rather less than human has to be suffered. The prelude to entering upon a new set of rules is a condition of being in which all restraints are cast off, desires satisfied. Men and women are as though free-movers in that golden age when no rules were necessary. And because it so easily can be, such a condition is often exemplified or realized by giving free rein to the sexual impulse: the first and primary impulse to be put under moral restraint if an ordered community life is to be made possible. Knox's remarks concerning the alternations of scandal and rigorism characteristic of enthusiastic movements are not simply good history. The two go together, are integral parts of a transition process in which the new rules are still experimental, uncertain. The interplay between the antitheses produces the synthesis.

It could be argued that orgies of sexual promiscuity—or indulging any of those other impulses (such as uncontrolled weeping, sobbing, wild dancing, writhing, flopping, hysteria, trance, speaking in tongues or shouting obscenities) whose expression evokes the antithesis of the ordered human frame— and the high idealism often connoted by the release from all desire, are polar opposites. But the fact remains that both meet in precisely the same condition: that of no obligation. Saint Paul's strictures on the sexual activities of his fellow Christians reveal not so much the prig as an awareness of what was involved in becoming free after moral awareness has cramped instinctual behaviour. In emphasizing a freedom of the spirit in the kingdom of Heaven, and propagating rules for the

guidance of the flesh, he drew an implicit distinction between
the two expressions of 'no rules'. Nor was Saint Paul the only
prophet to have trouble with this phase of 'no rules'. Few have
been able to resist the temptation to succumb themselves—Yali
and the Mahdi provide us with immediate instances—and most
have chosen the fleshly rather than spiritual expression of freedom from rules. In many movements it has been the disciples
and followers who have found that no rules can be profitable
as well as relaxing. And since it is difficult for a political regime
to reason with those who do not consider themselves bound by
rules, it is usually during this phase of no rules that, in the
colonial situation, an outraged administration feels bound to
take action. So too in other instances. Order cannot countenance
disorder.

In most revolutions there comes a point when, with the traditional structure of rules or values destroyed, power and the
struggle to gain it are subject to no rules or conventions. This is
the crucial phase, the naked struggle for power whose outcome
determines the course the revolution will take. In the same
way, before the new rules of a millenarian movement can
become firm, a phase of no rules has to be suffered. But it also
involves a struggle for power. Given the millenarian ambience
and locally acceptable modes of gaining a divine revelation
almost anyone might be a prophet and trigger off activities of a
millenarian kind. But the crucial moment comes when the
phase of no rules is entered. This is a prophet's real testing
ground. Whatever signs he may have provided, no matter how
glowing his eyes or wondrous his miracles, if he cannot retain
command and wring order out of anomy he fails to fulfil
himself wholly. He becomes another false prophet.

Once the prophet's claims have been found wanting, disciples
and followers may attempt to take over. But they tend to
compete with each other, and they do not have that initial elan
and charisma which comes from a divine revelation. The embryo
movement loses momentum. Either the power that is there
cannot be grasped by any of those involved, or there is no
real power to be grasped. The activities flicker on for a while,
then die. If some of the participants appear disillusioned, others
remain determined and, providing that the millenarian ambience persists, await the emergence of a more adequate prophet.

The third phase of the cyclical pattern is entered, and this may soon develop into the first.[1]

The phase for which we have the most evidence is that of anomy, no rules. And it is initiated by events which manifest an uncontrolled or uncontrollable power: flood or famine, a raging epidemic or hopeless war, the intrusion of foreigners or their ideas and things, disenfranchisement—our four situations and twelve oppositions. But though being underprivileged or deprived, or unable to understand or command their own fates, may drive men to desperate measures; and passionate though they may be in their resentments or in their more positive aspirations; they fail if their new rules cannot survive the passage of no rules. If the new rules are merely a slight qualification of the old rules they hardly deserve a millenarian frame. This demands a new beginning, a new whole-status with appropriate rules which transcends the old. If the new rules are fantasies they cannot be grasped and implemented. If the new rules are practicable and workable they can only be realized if there exist people sufficiently capable of making them work. If the new rules are worth having they must survive the test of no rules and, together with a consensus as to their content, there must be people capable of giving them an organizational framework and operating them. As in all interregnums, power awaits those who can show themselves capable of exercising it.

The diagram on the next page illustrates the main outlines of the argument.

[1] Above, p. 140.

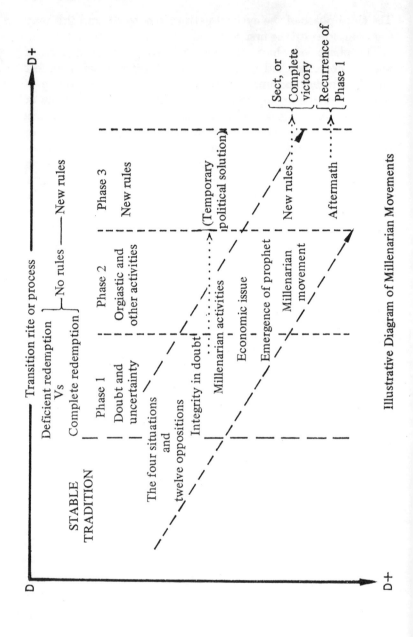

Illustrative Diagram of Millenarian Movements

13
Conclusion

We started this essay with three questions. Then, taking a statement by Haddon as a convenient point of departure for answering the questions, we went on to discuss its implications. Religion was defined as a set of basic assumptions about the ordering of power which guaranteed the rules of a redemptive process; this last was broken down into particular kinds of relations between prestige, status, integrity, and moral obligation. We have examined varieties of millenarian activity and discussed the problems they posed.

The first question was: What is the meaning of the millennium to those who participate in millenarian activities? The short answer is: A new situation and status which, providing the basis of a new integrity, will enable life to be lived more abundantly. The action involved in bringing about the new situation, it was suggested, could be understood in the terms of a synthesis which, in the broadest sense, derived from a loss of integrity and an unsatisfactory redemptive process on the one hand, and a vision of complete integrity and total redemption on the other. Where millenarian movements are concerned, status is not simply a matter of the pecking order, or of a hierarchy of ranks or socio-economic classes. It is a matter of acknowledged prestige and integrity, of being human, moral, and aspiring to fulfil the quality of one's humanity.

The second and third questions concerned methods of analysis and the search for sociological explanation. Here the dilemma was that explanation entailed becoming involved in competing millenarisms and thus in finding a unity and synthesis between opposed modes of understanding. This was exactly the dilemma of the millenarian situation itself. To resolve this dilemma, to rationalize the action in terms which subsumed the particular rationalizations of local cultural idioms, we examined

a variety of situations concerned with power and its transmission. Power, it was suggested, referring to our definition of
religion, cannot be allowed to run wild; it must be comprehended and controlled. And efforts to comprehend and control
power were triggered by circumstances summed up in terms of
four primary situations and twelve oppositions.[1] These set the
scene for millenarian activities.

With the anomic scene set, however, the curtain may go up to
reveal a mêlée of actors looking for their proper parts. For the
action to become coherent a prophet is necessary. He focuses
attention on the meaning of the millennium and brings order to
the inchoate activities. A bundle of particular kinds of social
experience, he succeeds or fails to fulfil his role in terms of
his own personal qualities, the content of his revelation, and the
history and experience of the people to whom he communicates.
He claims to be able to realize and order the power which seems
currently unrealized and unordered; the new ordering promises
a satisfactory way of measuring meaningful qualities, a new
redemptive process. Given that, as an experiment in finding new
ways, a millenarian movement never fails entirely, a prophet
may succeed in developing the movement into a dissident sect,

[1] The only alternative to attempting to comprehend and control
power brought within the range of apprehension is, it seems, to shut
one's eyes to it. On sighting an aircraft a New Guinea people engaged in
millenarian activities. But the first Australians to encounter Captain
Cook's ship did not perceive it until, seeing human beings somewhat like
themselves disembarking from it, they were forced to try and comprehend both the ship and its crew. (See *Moorehead*, p. 104, quoting Sir
Sidney Parkinson. Compare also the New Guinean who perceived in a
photograph what the photographer never saw, above, p. 61, n. 1.)

From the moment they perceived the ship, given the alternatives of
adhering to traditional ways or accommodating new kinds of power,
millenarian activities among Australian aborigines became possible. As
matter of history they chose, or were forced into, the first alternative.
Recently, however, the second alternative has become a realizable
possibility. With tradition found wanting, or impractical, millenarian
activities have begun.

In the case of one of these movements (*Berndt* (3)), Professor Berndt
informs me, the activities have settled to a routine. It is run by a particularly lively prophet-secretary. Negotiations with the political regime
are handled in an orderly way through joint meetings and the exchange
of letters. The prophet-secretary conducts his business with his own
typewriter.

quietist or more militant, or, more rarely, the energies he releases may so develop as to take over complete control. On the other hand, the prophet may fail. The amount of power thought available may be an illusion. Because the new measures of worth tend to hinge on the handling of money, a sophisticated exercise, prophet and followers may founder in ignorance. Or the movement may peter out in the marshes of uncertainty and conflicting interests.

The phase of no rules through which a millenarian movement passes invites opposition from outside and also engenders an internal struggle for power. But these do not necessarily offset each other. Outside opposition may exacerbate internal dissidence. Though a prophet's inspiration is in itself singular, it is understood as demanding binary discriminations, reciprocity of obligation, no rights without enforceable obligations. In their nature as moral beings, humans resent the presence of unenforceable obligations. On the other hand, because they are human, men are quick to seize upon privilege and, imitating the free-movers of myth and the heart's desire, they are not slow to unburden themselves of obligation if they can. That singular exercise of power exampled in the prophet's inspiration is in all men in some part. If the tendency of power to concentrate and become absolute is constantly countered by the struggle to diffuse it among larger numbers of persons, still, as power is diffused so do the more competent take it from those less able to exercise it. And as increasing numbers of people are enabled to disregard their obligations with impunity, so previously held assumptions about the exercise and control of power begin to wither in doubt and uncertainty. Men rally to those new assumptions which look as though they will control and redistribute the power available, which will satisfactorily measure the qualities they believe they have. And they are likely to do so in terms of those exacting binary discriminations which the use of money tends to deny.

Works Cited

ALLAN, C. H. 'A Nativistic Cult in the British Solomon Islands', *South Pacific* July, 1951, Vol. 5, No. 5, pp. 79–85.

ANDREWS, Edward Deming. *The People Called Shakers*, New York, 1963.

BABBAGE, S. B. *Hauhauism*, New Zealand, 1937.

BALANDIER, Georges. 'Messianismes et nationalismes en Afrique Noire', *Cahiers Internationales de Sociologie*, Vol. XIV, 8e année, Paris, 1953.

BARNETT, H. G. *Indian Shakers: A Messianic Cult of the Pacific Northwest*, Southern Illinois U.P., 1957.

BASHAM, A. L. *The Wonder that was India*, London, 1954.

BEATTIE, J. H. M. 'Ritual and Social Change', *Man* Vol. 1, No. 1, March 1966, pp. 60–71.

BEAUVOIR, Simone de. *The Second Sex*, New York, London, 1965.

BELSHAW, C. S.
  (1) 'The Significance of Modern Cults in Melanesian Development', *The Australian Outlook* Vol. IV, June, 1950, pp. 116–25.
  (2) *Changing Melanesia*, Melbourne, 1950.

BERNDT, R. M.
  (1) 'The Influence of European Culture on Australian Aborigines', *Oceania* Vol. XXI, No. 3, 1951.
  (2) 'A Cargo Movement in the Central Highlands of New Guinea', *Oceania* Vol. XXIII, 1952, pp. 40–65, 137–58, 202–34.
  (3) *An Adjustment Movement in Arnhem Land, Northern Territory of Australia*, Paris, 1962.

BEST, Elsdon. *Maori Religion and Mythology*, Wellington, 1924.

BREWSTER, A. B. *The Hill Tribes of Fiji*, London, 1922.

BREWSTER, E. W. *The Life of Gautama the Buddha*, London, 1926.

BROWNE, E. G. *The Babi Religion*, Cambridge, 1918.

BRUIJN, J. V. de. 'The Mansren Cult of Biak', *South Pacific* Vol. V, No. 1, 1951, pp. 1–10.

BURRIDGE, Kenelm (K.O.L.).

(1) 'Cargo Cult Activity in Tangu', *Oceania* XXIV, 1954,p p. 241–53.

(2) 'Racial Tension in Manam', *South Pacific* Vol. 7, No. 13, 1954, pp. 932–8.

(3) *Mambu: A Melanesian Millennium*, London, 1960.

(4) 'Kuda Kepang in Batu Pahat, Johore', *Man* 26 February, 1961.

(5) 'Tangu, Northern Madang District', in *Gods, Ghosts and Men in Melanesia* (Eds. P. Lawrence and M. J. Meggitt), pp. 224–49, O.U.P., Melbourne, 1965.

BUTT, A. J. 'The Birth of a Religion', *Journal of the Royal Anthropological Institute*, Vol. 90, Pt 1, pp. 66–106.

CAPELL, A. 'The word "mana" : A linguistic study', *Oceania*, Vol. IX, 1939, pp. 89–126.

CHINNERY, E. W. P. and HADDON, A. C. 'Five New Religious Cults in British New Guinea' *The Hibbert Journal*, Vol. XV, No. 3, 1917, pp. 448–63.

COHN, Norman. *The Pursuit of the Millennium*, London, 1957.

COWAN, James. *The New Zealand Wars and the Pioneering Period*, Vol. II, Wellington, N.Z., 1923.

CROCOMBE, R. G. 'A Modern Polynesian Cargo Cult', *Man* 28, February, 1961.

CROOME, Honor. *Introduction to Money*, London, 1962.

CROWTHER, G. *An Outline of Money*, London, 1955.

DALTON, G.

(1) 'Economic Theory and Primitive Society', *American Anthropologist*, Vol. 63, 1961, pp. 1–23.

(2) 'Primitive Money', *American Anthropologist* Vol. 67, 1965, pp. 44–65.

DAVENPORT, W. 'When a Primitive and Civilized Money Meet', *Proceedings of the American Ethnological Spring Meeting Symposium*, 1961.

DOZIER, Edward P. 'Rio Grande Pueblos' in *Perspectives in American Indian Culture Change* (Ed. Edward H. Spicer), pp. 94–186. University of Chicago Press, 1961.

EINZIG, Paul. *Primitive Money* (revised edition), London, 1966.

EKKA, Philip. *The Tana Bhagats: A study in social change* (Oxford). Unpublished D.Phil. thesis, 1966.

ELLIS, William. *Polynesian Researches*, 2 volumes, London, 1929.

EMMETT, Dorothy. 'Prophets and their Societies', *Journal of the Royal Anthropological Institute*, Vol. 86, 1956, pp. 13–23.

EVANS-PRITCHARD, E. E.

    (1) *The Nuer*, Oxford, 1940.

    (2) 'Social Anthropology: Past and Present' (The Marett Lecture, 1950) Reprinted in *Essays in Social Anthropology*, London, 1962, pp. 13–28.

    (3) *Nuer Religion*, Oxford, 1956.

EWERS, John C. *The Blackfeet*, University of Oklahoma Press, 1961.

FIRTH, Raymond.

    (1) *Primitive Economics of the New Zealand Maori*, London, 1929.

    (2) *Primitive Polynesian Economy*, London, 1939.

    (3) 'The analysis of mana: an empirical study', *Journal of the Polynesian Society*, Vol. 49, 1940, pp. 483–510.

    (4) *The Work of the Gods in Tikopia*, London, 1940.

    (5) *Elements of Social Organization*, London, 1951.

    (6) (and Yamey, B. S.) *Capital, Saving and Credit in Peasant Societies*, 1964.

FITZGERALD, C. P.

    (1) *China*, London, 1935.

    (2) *China: A Short Cultural History* (2nd Ed.), London, 1958.

FREEMAN, J. D. 'The Joe Gimlet or Siovili Cult' in *Anthropology in the South Seas* (Eds. J. D. Freeman and W. R. Geddes), New Plymouth, New Zealand, 1959, pp. 185–99.

FUCHS, Stephen. *Rebellious Prophets*, Bombay, 1965.

GENNEP, Arnold Van. *The Rites of Passage*, first published 1908. Translation by Monika Brizedom and Gabrielle L. Caffee. Routledge and Kegan Paul, London, 1960.

GODELIER, M. 'Objet et Methodes de l'Anthropologie Economique' *L'Homme*, Vol. V, No. 2, 1965, pp. 33–91.

GOLDSCHMIDT, Walter. *Comparative Functionalism*, University of California Press, 1966.

GOULD, Julius, and KOLB, William L. *A Dictionary of the Social Sciences*, London, 1964.

GRAZIA, Sebastian de. *The Political Community*, University of Chicago Press, Chicago, 1948.

GREENWOOD, William. 'The Upraised Hand', *Journal of the Polynesian Society* Vol. 51, 1942, pp. 1–81.

GUDGEON, W. E. 'Mana Tangata', *Journal of the Polynesian Society* Vol. 14, 1905, pp. 49–66.

GUIART, Jean.
(1) 'Cargo Cults and Political Evolution in Melanesia', *Mankind*, Vol. 4, No. 6, 1951, pp. 227–9.
(2) 'Forerunners of Melanesian Nationalism', *Oceania*, Vol. XXII, 1951, pp. 81–90.
(3) *Les Religions de l'Océanie*, Paris, 1962.

GUNTHER, E. 'The Shaker Religion of the Northwest' in *Indians of the Urban Northwest* (Ed. M. W. Smith), pp. 37–76, New York, 1949.

HARROP, A. J. *England and the Maori Wars*, London, 1937.

HILL, W. 'The Navaho Indians and the Ghost Dance of 1890', *American Anthropologist* Vol. XLVI, 1944, p. 523.

HOEBEL, E. A.
(1) 'The Comanche Sun Dance and Messianic Outbreak of 1873', *American Anthropologist* Vol. XLIII, 1941, pp. 301–3.
(2) *The Cheyennes*, New York, 1960.

HOGBIN, H. IAN. 'Mana', *Oceania* Vol. VI, No. 3, March 1936, pp. 241–74.

HÖLTKER, Georg. 'Die Mambu Bewegung in Neuguinea: ein Beitrag zum Prophetentum in Melanesien', *Annali Lateranensi* Tom V. 181–219, 1941.

HONIGMANN, John J. 'Social Networks in Great Whale River', *National Museum of Canada, Bulletin* No. 178, 1962.

HORTON, Robin. 'A Definition of Religion, and its Uses', *Journal of the Royal Anthropological Institute*, Vol. 90, Pt 2, pp. 201–226.

INGLIS, Judy. 'Cargo Cults: The Problem of Explanation', *Oceania*, Vol. XXVII, No. 4, 1957, pp. 249–63.

JAINI, Jagmanderlal. *Outlines of Jainism*, Cambridge, 1940.

JARVIE, I. C.
(1) 'Theories of Cargo Cults: A Critical Analysis' *Oceania*, Vol. XXXIV, No. 1, Sept., pp. 1–31; No. 2, Dec., 1963, pp. 109–36.
(2) *The Revolution in Anthropology*, London, 1964.

    (3) 'On the Explanation of Cargo Cults', *European Journal of Sociology* Vol. VII, 1966, pp. 299–312.

KAMINSKY, Howard. 'The Problem of Explanation' in *Millennial Dreams in Action* (Ed. Sylvia Thrupp), pp. 215–17, Mouton, The Hague, 1962.

KEMPIS, Thomas à. *The Imitation of Christ.* Everyman's Library, J. M. Dent & Sons, London, 1928.

KNOX, R. A. *Enthusiasm*, Oxford, 1950.

KOESTLER, Arthur. *The Act of Creation*, Pan Books Limited, London, 1966 (originally published 1964).

LAMB, Harold.
    (1) *Genghis Khan, Emperor of all Men*, London, 1927.
    (2) *Tamerlane: the Earth Shaker*, London, 1932.

LANGEWIS, L. 'Lamak and Malat in Bali', *Royal Tropical Institute*, Amsterdam, No. CXIX, 1956, pp. 37–45, esp. p. 31.

LANTERNARI, Vittorio. *The Religions of the Oppressed* (first published 1960). Mentor Books, New York, 1965.

LAWRENCE, Peter.
    (1) 'Cargo Cult and Religious beliefs among the Garia', *International Archives of Ethnography*, Vol. XLVII, No. 1, 1954, pp. 1–20.
    (2) *Road Belong Cargo*, Manchester, 1964.

LAWRENCE, Peter and MEGGITT, M. J. (Eds.) *Gods, Ghosts and Men in Melanesia*, Melbourne (O.U.P.), 1965.

LEACH, E. R.
    (1) *Political Systems of Highland Burma*, London, 1954.
    (2) *Rethinking Anthropology*, London, 1963.

LESSER, A. 'Cultural Significance of the Ghost Dance', *American Anthropologist*, Vol. XXXV, 1933, pp. 108–15.

LÉVI-STRAUSS, Claude.
    (1) *Structural Anthropology*, New York, 1963, London, 1968.
    (2) *The Savage Mind*, London, 1966.

LEWIS, I. M. 'Spirit Possession and Deprivation Cults', *Man* Vol. I, No. 3, Sept., 1966, pp. 307–29.

LIENHARDT, R. G. 'Religion' (in *Man, Culture and Society*. Ed. H. L. Shapiro), New York, 1956, pp. 310–29.

LINTON, R. 'Nativistic Movements', *American Anthropologist* Vol. XLV, 1943, pp. 230–40.

LOMMEL, A. 'Modern Cultural Influences on the Aborigines', *Oceania* Vol. XXI, No. 1, 1950.

MACAULIFFE, Max Arthur. *The Sikh Religion* Vol. VI, O.U.P., New Delhi, 1963 (reprinted).

MARTINDALE, Don. (Ed.) *Functionalism in Social Science* (American Academy of Political and Social Science. Monograph 5), Philadelphia, 1965.

MATHIASSEN, THERKEL. *The Material Culture of the Iglulik Eskimos*. Reports of the Fifth Thule Expedition, Vol. 6, Denmark, 1928.

MATTHEWS, Ronald. *English Messiahs*, London, 1936.

MILLER, R. FULOP-. *Leaders, Dreamers and Rebels*, Harrap, London, 1935.

MOONEY, James. *The Ghost Dance Religion and the Sioux outbreak of 1890* (Anthony F. Wallace, Ed.), University of Chicago Press, London, 1965 (1896).

MOOREHEAD, Alan. *The Fatal Impact*, London, 1966.

MUKERJEE, Radhakamal. *The Social Structure of Values*, London, 1950.

OWEN, A. L. *The Famous Druids*, Oxford, 1962.

PARSONS, Elsie Clew. *Pueblo Indian Religion*, University of Chicago Press, 1939.

PIDDINGTON, Ralph. *An Introduction to Social Anthropology*, Vol. 2, London, Oliver and Boyd, 1957.

POCOCK, D. F. *Social Anthropology*, Sheed and Ward, London, 1961.

QUEIROZ, Maria Isaura Pereira de. *O Messianismo no Brasil e no Mundo*, Universidade de São Paolo, São Paolo, 1965.

ROGERS, P. G. *The Fifth Monarchy Men*, O.U.P., London, 1966.

ROY, S. C.
   (1) 'A New Religious Movement Among the Oraons', *Man in India*, Vol. 1, No. 4, 1921, pp. 267–324.
   (2) *Oraon Religion and Customs* (pp. 312–410), Ranchi and Calcutta, 1928.

SADLER, A. L. *A Short History of Japan*, Sydney, 1962 (2nd ed.).

SANSOM, G. B. *Japan, A Short Cultural History*, London, 1962 (revised edition).

SARGANT, William. *Battle for the Mind*, Pan Books, London, 1957 (1963).

SCHAPERA, I. 'Should Anthropologists be Historians?', *Journal of the Royal Anthropological Institute* Vol. 92, 1962, Part 2, pp. 143–56. Presidential Address.

SCHOLEM, Gersholm G. *On the Kabbalah and its Symbolism*, London, 1965.

SERRIN, O. 'The Bhagat Movement in Chota Nagpur', *Indian Academy*, Kurseny, 1917.

SMITH, Marian W.
  (1) 'Shamanism in the Shaker Religion of the Northwest', *Man*, 181, August, 1954.
  (2) 'Towards a Classification of Cult Movements', *Man*, 2, January, 1959.

STANNER, W. E. H. 'On the Interpretation of Cargo Cults', *Oceania* Vol. XXIX, No. 1, Sept., 1958, pp. 1–25.

STEVENSON, Mrs. Sinclair. *The Heart of Jainism*, 1915.

STEINER, Franz. 'Notes on Comparative Economics', *British Journal of Sociology* Vol. 5, 1954, pp. 118–29.

SUNDKLER, Bengt G. M. *Bantu Prophets in South Africa*, Lutterworth Press, London, 1948.

THOMAS, E. J. *The Life of Buddha: As Legend and History* (2nd ed.), London, 1930.

THRUPP, Sylvia L. (ed.) *Millennial Dreams in Action*, Mouton, The Hague, 1962.

TREGEAR, Edward. 'The Pai-Marire word *Hau*', *Journal of the Polynesian Society* Vol. XIII, 1904, p. 193.

TYLOR, Sir Edward Burnett. *Primitive Culture* (2 vols.), London, 1891.

VERNON, Glenn M. *Sociology of Religion*, McGraw Hill, New York, 1962.

VOGET, Fred W. 'The American Indian in Transition: Reformation and Accommodation', *American Anthropologist* Vol. LVIII, 1956, pp. 249–63.

WALLACE, Anthony F. C. 'Revitalization Movements', *American Anthropologist* Vol. LVIII, 1956, pp. 264–81.

WEBER, Max. *The Theory of Social and Economic Organization* (Ed. Talcott Parsons), Free Press, Glencoe, 1964 (1947).

WALLIS, Wilson D. *Messiahs: Christian and Pagan*, Boston, The Gorham Press, 1918.

WILSON, Bryan. *Sects and Society*, London, 1961.

WILLIAMS, F. E.
  (1) *The Vailala Madness and the Destruction of Native Ceremonies in the Gulf Division*, Port Moresby, 1923.
  (2) *Orokaiva Magic*, London, O.U.P., 1928.

(3) 'The Vailala Madness in Retrospect' in Evans-Pritchard, E. E., *et al. Essays presented to C. G. Seligman*, London, 1934.

WILLIAMS, Herbert W. *A Dictionary of the Maori Language*, Wellington, New Zealand, 1917.

WILLIAMSON, R. W.

(1) *Religious and Cosmic Beliefs of Central Polynesia* 2 vols., Cambridge, 1933.

(2) *Religion and Social Organization in Central Polynesia* (Ed. R. Piddington), Cambridge, 1937.

WINKS, Robin W. 'The Doctrine of Hauhauism', *Journal of the Polynesian Society* Vol. 62, No. 3, 1953, pp. 199–237.

WORSLEY, Peter. *The Trumpet Shall Sound*, London, 1957. Revised edition, 1968.

YINGER, Milton. *Religion, Society and the Individual*, New York, 1957.

Index

accommodative (cult or movement), 102

adjustment (cult or movement), 102

administration, 9, 15, 18, 26–8, 36, 45, 48, 51, 54–5, 58–68, 84–8, 101, 123, 128–9, 132, 152

Administrator, the, 54

Africa(n), 3, 33, 101, 137

aftermath, 112, 170

ahimsa, 93–4

aircraft, 35, 37n., 62, 143–5, 152n.

Aitape, 57

Aladdin, 159

Allan, C. H., 120n.

America(n), 38, 59, 66, 101, 137
  North, 57, 76, 86
  South, 33, 57

ancestors, 6, 20, 64–6, 82

Andrews, E. D., 94n.

angels, 5, 16–17, 21, 31
  Angel Gabriel, 16, 19, 108

anomy, 37–8, 169, 172

antinomianism, 128

anxiety, 106, 121, 147
  Anxiety-Dream, 120
  Anxiety-Separation, 120

Asia(n), 33, 101, 137

aspirations, 67, 72, 90, 97

assumptions, 5–13, 21–30, 35–37, 41, 47–50, 55, 67, 74, 84–86, 95–7, 103, 106–8, 117, 121–4, 127, 140–2, 150–4, 162–3

Australia, 22, 67

Australian aborigines, 34, 39, 40, 59, 68, 112–13, 172n.

authenticity, 75, 82, 91, 158, 163

authority, 14, 31–2, 47–52, 54–56, 61, 75, 82, 91, 107–9, 123, 132, 142, 152–8

Babbage, S. B., 15, 17n.

Baigona (cult or movement), 55–6, 62, 87n., 102

Balandier, G., 33n.

baptism, 27–8, 61, 112

Barnett, H. G., 33n., 103n.

Basham, A. L., 87n.

Beattie, J. H. M., 120n., 121n.

Beauvoir, Simone de, 42n.

being (condition of), 6, 10, 11, 27, 41, 55–8, 68, 71, 95, 102, 106, 112, 129, 135, 141, 161–162

Belshaw, C. S., 122n., 128n.

Berndt, R. M., 35n., 39n., 102n., 172n.

Best, E., 28n.

Gaugin, Paul, 39
Gautama Buddha, 87–94, 102
genie, 159–60
Genesis, 51
Gennep, Arnold van, 166n.
German(s)(y), 57, 59
gestalt, 139
Ghengis Khan, 33
ghost, 5, 53
Ghost Dance Religion, 78–82
God, 7, 22, 57, 71, 89, 99, 101,
   118, 125, 137–8, 142
Godelier, M., 42n.
gods, 28, 70, 118, 162
Goldschmidt, Walter, 2n.
Gould, Julius, 103n.
government, 18, 32–4, 38–42,
   95, 105–6, 133
governor, 18, 24–5, 54
Grace, 127–8
Grazia, Sebastian de, 120n.
Greenwood, William, 15, 21n.
Gudgeon, W. E., 20n.
Guiart, Jean, 28n.
Gunther, E., 33n.
guru, 91, 150

Haddon, A. C., 3, 4, 9, 10, 53,
   54n., 55n., 95
Ham, 71
Harrop, A. J., 15n., 16n., 18n.,
   19n.
Hauhau (cult or movement),
   15, 16, 18–21
heaven, 19, 50, 79, 81
Hegel, G. W. Friedrich, 2n.
'Hegelian' explanation, 118,
   136–40
hell fire, 4, 50, 134
hero, 10, 11, 51, 60, 67

hierarchy, 93, 113, 123, 142,
   151
Hill, W., 33n.
Hindu, 83–5, 87–96, 108
Hoebel, A. J., 80n.
Hogbin, H. Ian, 20n.
holocaust, 65
Höltker, Georg, 65n.
Holy Spirit, 131
Honigman, John J., 33n.
horse, 75–8, 88
Horton, Robin, 7
human nature, 140, 162
hymns, 17, 24, 38, 54
hysteria, 10

iconoclasm, 33, 36
incest taboo, 112, 166
India, 33, 83
Inglis, Judy, 117n., 121n.
inspiration, 12, 37, 55, 57, 82,
   101, 117, 131, 155–6
integrity, 11, 13, 20–6, 30, 35,
   39, 46, 61, 69, 74, 75–97,
   106–8, 110, 122, 163–4
intellect, 64, 71–2, 107, 109–
   110
invulnerability, 17, 19, 21, 39,
   50, 76, 79, 112, 134
Irakau, 59–61, 72n.
irrational, 7, 117, 123–4, 129
Islam, 11, 32–3, 161

Jain(s)(ism), 33, 86–96, 102,
   108, 143, 146
Jaini, Jagmanderlal, 33n., 87n.
Japan(ese), 33, 59, 66, 72
Jarvie, I. C., 2n., 117n.
Jehovah, 118
Jesu Kerisu, 53

The Alphabet Garden